LEVEL D

Comprehension PLUS

Dr. Diane Lapp
Dr. James Flood

Modern Curriculum Press

All photos ©Pearson Learning unless otherwise noted.

Photographs

5: Dave B. Fleetham/Tom Stack & Assoc. 6: Kelvin Aitken/Peter Arnold, Inc. 8: Michael DeMocker/Visuals Unlimited. 9: Courtesy of George Greenwood. 13: Bettman-Corbis. 14: AP/Wide World. 29-30, 62 t.l., 63: NASA. 33: David Neel. 34: t.r. Nathan Benn/Corbis-Bettman. 34: m.b. Robert Frerck/Odyssey. 36: Corbis. 42: Cindy Charles/PhotoEdit. 45: Jules Frazier/PhotoDisc, Inc. 46: m.b. Courtesy of Midori & Friends. 46: t.r. Susan Johann. 49: Brown Brothers. 50:, Lawrence Migdale/Photo Researchers, Inc. 61: The Granger Collection. 62: Corbis. 65: Jonathan Blair/National Geographic Society Image Sales. 66: Morgol Nicol-Hathaway/Whydah Society. 69: m.l., Renee Lynn/Photo Researchers, Inc. 69: m.r. Tom Brakefield/The Stock Market. 70: Santokh Kochar/PhotoDisc, Inc. 89, 94 b., 109: SuperStock, Inc. 93: Phil Degginger/Bruce Coleman, Inc. 96, 102: b.r. PhotoDisc, Inc. 96: t.r. Stone. 97: Tim Flach/Stone. 101: John Warden/Stone. 102: Alan & Sandy Carey/PhotoDisc, Inc. 110: Merlin D. Tuttle/Bat Conservation International. 112: Dr. Peter Vogel/Université de Lausanne. 114: Michael Newman/PhotoEdit. 117: Hugh Sitton/Stone. 118: Art Wolfe/Stone. 121: J. Patronite/Allsport Photography. 122: Duomo. 124: David Madison/Duomo

Illustrations

10, 12: Pam Tanzey. 18, 20: Diana Magnuson. 21-22: Dennis Hockerman. 26: Roberta Collier Morales. 37, 38: b., t.r. Gary Torrisi. 41: Doris Ettlinger. 53-54: Jane Kendall. 57-58: Meg Aubrey. 73-74, 76: Jane McCreary. 77-78: Diana Thewlis. 82: Antonio Castro. 86: Roger Roth. 98: Deborah White.

Cover art: photo montage: Wendy Wax. background: Doug Bowles.

Design development: MKR Design, New York: Manuela Paul, Deirdre Newman, Marta K. Ruliffson.

Design: Stephen Barth

ISBN: 0-7652-2183-7
Printed in the United States of America

27 20

1-800-321-3106
www.pearsonlearning.com

Table of Contents

Comprehending Text

Story Structure

Word Study

Document Reading

Main Idea and Details

If someone asked you what a paragraph or article was about, you would tell what the **topic** was in a word or two. If someone asked you what the **main idea** was, you would tell the most important idea about the topic. When you look for the main idea, you may find it in a sentence in the passage. If the main idea is not given, you have to figure it out and tell it in your own words. Knowing the main idea helps you better understand what you read. Other sentences in a passage usually contain **supporting details** that tell more about the main idea.

Read the following paragraph about the octopus. As you read, think about the topic, the main idea, and supporting details.

Some people may think the octopus is a strange and scary creature when they see its eight snakelike arms. The octopus's tentacles are actually useful tools. They help the octopus crawl along and explore the ocean floor. The octopus also uses its tentacles to hunt for food. Lining each tentacle are two rows of strong, circular suckers. The octopus can quickly grab and hold a small fish or crab with the suckers while stunning it with a poisonous bite. Losing a tentacle is not a problem for an octopus. It just grows a replacement.

On the chart below, write the topic and the sentence from the passage that tells the main idea. Then write two supporting details.

TOPIC: _____

Main Idea: _____
Detail: _____   _____
Detail: _____   _____

Tip

The main idea is the most important idea. Details support the main idea. To check yourself, ask, "Do all the important details tell about the main idea?"

On Your Own

As you read the following article about sharks, think about the topic. Then look for the main idea and supporting details in each paragraph.

The Great White Shark: The Hungry Hunter

While ocean divers work to film a school of fish, one diver feels a tug on her safety line. Another diver is pointing at a great white shark moving toward them. The shark moves in circles, but the experienced divers stay calm. They know that sharks rarely attack humans. The divers move closer together, though, since a shark is more likely to attack a lone swimmer. The shark slowly circles again, and then swims away.

Great white sharks are misunderstood creatures. Many people think that they are cruel, bloodthirsty killers out to harm them. Experts, however, believe that these sharks kill because they are always hungry. Humans are not sharks' usual food. In fact, once they bite into humans, great white sharks usually spit them out. Millions of people swim in the oceans, but sharks hardly ever consider them as prey.

A closer inspection of a great white shark will explain why it is so greatly feared. The shark has a mouth full of razor-sharp teeth, sometimes five rows of them. An adult shark often stretches 18 feet long and weighs close to 3,500 pounds. The largest recorded great white shark was 21 feet long and weighed 7,000 pounds!

The great white shark can smell a tiny amount of blood in the water and trace it to a wounded animal. It can see its prey from as far away as 30 to 40 feet. Small holes on the shark's snout also sense signals from other creatures. These signals lead the shark straight to its next meal. The gray-and-white color of its skin helps the shark to blend into the background and allows it to sneak up on its victims. Large muscles help it to swim quickly to find the food it senses.

Checking Comprehension

1. What misunderstanding do people have about the great white shark?

   _____

   _____

2. What is the most likely reason for a shark to attack a human?

   _____

Practicing Comprehension Skills

3. Fill in the circle next to the topic of the passage.

   ○ ocean divers   ○ great white sharks   ○ a school of fish   ○ marine seals

Read the following sentences. Write **MI** next to the main idea of each paragraph. Write **SD** next to each supporting detail.

Paragraph 1

4. _____ Ocean divers stay calm when a great white shark appears.

5. _____ The divers move closer together.

6. _____ The divers know that sharks rarely attack humans.

Paragraph 2

7. _____ Great white sharks are misunderstood creatures.

8. _____ Experts believe these sharks kill because they are always hungry.

9. _____ Humans are not sharks' usual food.

Paragraph 3

10. _____ The shark has a mouth full of razor sharp teeth.

11. _____ A closer inspection of a great white shark will explain why it is so greatly feared.

12. _____ A great white can be 18 feet long and weigh close to 3,500 pounds.

13. Reread the last paragraph of the article. Complete the following diagram. Write the main idea at the top. Then write four details that support the main idea.

Main Idea: _____	
Detail: _____ _____	Detail: _____ _____
Detail: _____ _____	Detail: _____ _____

Practicing Vocabulary

Match the word on the left with the word or words on the right that mean the same thing. Write the letter on the line.

_____ 14. bloodthirsty   **a.** hurt

_____ 15. harm   **b.** animal captured for food

_____ 16. misunderstood   **c.** nose

_____ 17. shark   **d.** big type of fish

_____ 18. prey   **e.** cruel

_____ 19. experienced   **f.** skillful

_____ 20. snout   **g.** seen incorrectly

MAKING THE **Reading** AND **Writing** CONNECTION

Writing an Informative Paragraph
Choose an animal such as the great white shark that you think is interesting. On a separate sheet of paper, write a paragraph describing the animal. Write a main idea sentence. Then write supporting details. Include a title that gives the topic.

Drawing Conclusions

As you read a story or an article, you may need to figure out some things that the author doesn't tell you. Look for and think about details that the author gives you. Then combine those details with what you know from your own experiences to make a decision or **draw a conclusion.**

Drawing conclusions helps you better understand the things that happen in a story or an article. Your conclusions will also help you know how characters or people feel and why they act the way they do.

Read the following article. Use information in the article and what you know to draw conclusions about the people and events.

Young Chester Greenwood had a problem. He lived in Farmington, Maine, where cold winter temperatures turned his tender ears red, purple, and blue. Unfortunately, wool scarves made Chester's ears itch.

One winter in 1873, Chester gathered wire from the barn. He found beaver fur and velvet in his mother's sewing basket. His grandmother helped him put them together. That's how Chester invented the Greenwood Champion Ear Protector. His invention was an instant hit and soon warmed ears throughout Farmington.

By the 1880s, Chester was wealthy. His popular invention became known as earmuffs. Farmington had become the earmuff capital of the world.

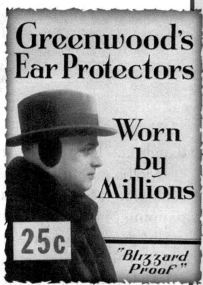

Greenwood's Ear Protectors

Worn by Millions

25c

"Blizzard Proof"

Tip

Use what you read and your own experiences to draw a conclusion. Test a conclusion using details in the story. Also ask yourself, "Does this conclusion make sense?"

Write your answer to the question on the lines.

Do you think other people had ear problems similar to Chester's? Why or why not?

_____

_____

Read the following story about an inventor. Use details and your own experiences to draw conclusions about the characters and story events.

Melba and the Magno-Doggie

"Melba!" Mrs. Washington called to her daughter. "Please take Arthur for a walk."

Melba groaned. It was rainy and muggy. As Melba looked down at the basset hound napping on the rug, Arthur lifted a baggy eyelid. Soon the pair were on their way, strolling along the wet pavement.

Arthur strained at his leash as they entered the soggy park. The park was deserted, so Melba removed the leash. Arthur dashed away.

Melba hollered a friendly, "Here, boy!" first and then a forceful, "Come, Arthur!" When neither call brought Arthur back, Melba was off on a canine chase. When she finally got Arthur back on his leash, he whined. Muddy girl and muddy dog trudged home, both in a bad mood.

Melba wanted her pet to be happy, so she thought about how to solve her problem. On her father's workbench, she laid out Arthur's dog collar, magnets, and some iron scraps. Melba started to work.

The next day, the Magno-Doggie was ready for a test. Melba and Arthur returned to the park. Melba unfastened the leash, and Arthur trotted off with a small piece of iron attached to his collar. Melba knew he wouldn't come back if she called, so she was ready with her equipment. From a belt pouch labeled "Magno-Doggie," Melba pulled out a colossal magnet and pointed it at Arthur.

Zzzzip! Arthur scooted backward across the grass. His physique was so low to the ground that he slid easily without falling over. He looked quite surprised as the magnetic force reeled him in like a fish.

A man sitting on a park bench called out, "That's a great invention!" Melba Washington was an inventor!

"Melba," Mrs. Washington called as dog and daughter returned, "please watch your brother while I run an errand. Don't let him wander!" With a gleam in her eye, Melba wondered if Darryl would mind a few scraps of iron glued to his belt.

Checking Comprehension

1. How does Melba's invention work?

   _____

   _____

2. What do you think Melba plans to do with the Magno-Doggie as
   the story ends?

   _____

   _____

Practicing Comprehension Skills

Fill in the circle next to the best answer to each question.

3. What conclusion can you draw about Arthur when he whined?
   - ○ Arthur doesn't like walks.   ○ Arthur doesn't like the leash.
   - ○ Arthur doesn't like Melba.   ○ Arthur has seen a bigger dog.

4. Why was Melba in a bad mood when she returned from
   the park the first time?
   - ○ It was a soggy day.   ○ Arthur whined the whole time.
   - ○ She had to chase Arthur through   ○ Her new invention had not
     the mud.   worked well.

5. Why is Melba Washington an inventor?
   - ○ Melba lets Arthur run at the park. ○ Melba walks the dog when her
                                             mother asks her to.
   - ○ Arthur runs away when Melba lets   ○ Melba creates a device that solves
     him off the leash.   a problem.

Write your answer to each question on the lines.

6. What conclusion can you draw about the kind of person Melba is?

   _____

7. What conclusion can you draw about how well Arthur is trained?

_____

_____

8. Write two details in the story that would help you conclude that Melba's invention is a success.

Detail: _____

Detail: _____

Practicing Vocabulary

Write the word from the box that belongs in each group.

colossal	equipment	errand	forceful	physique	pouch	reeled

9. bag, sack, _____

10. gigantic, enormous, _____

11. body, appearance, _____

12. strong, powerful, _____

13. pulled, dragged, _____

14. supplies, tools, _____

15. trip, outing, _____

Writing a Paragraph That Explains
With a partner, think of a problem like Melba's that needs solving. On another sheet of paper, draw a picture of an invention. On the paper's other side, describe the problem and how your invention will solve it.

Sequence: Order of Events

Sequence is the order in which events happen in a story. As you read, you may find words and phrases that will help you figure out the sequence. For example, words such as *first, then, later, Tuesday,* and *in the afternoon* tell when things happened. Dates tell you a specific month or year.

In some stories and articles, two or more events happen at the same time. Words such as *meanwhile* and *during* can be clues that more than one thing is happening at the same time. If there are no clue words, you need to ask yourself what happens *first, next,* and *last* to figure out a sequence that makes sense.

As you read the article, look for clue words and the order of events.

On December 1, 1955, an African-American woman named Rosa Parks was riding the bus home from work. A white man was standing up on the crowded bus. The driver demanded that Parks give up her seat. At the time, the law in many places in the South said African Americans had to give up their seats to white people. Rosa Parks refused to give up her seat. She was tired of giving in to laws that were unfair.

Parks was arrested and found guilty of disorderly conduct. Four days later, the Rev. Dr. Martin Luther King, Jr., organized a bus boycott. African Americans did not patronize city buses for over a year. Finally, the court ruled that African Americans no longer had to give up their seats to white people.

Write your answer to each question on the lines.

What words or phrases give clues about the sequence?

everything

What happened after Rosa Parks was arrested?

she went to jail

Tip

When you read, look for clue words and phrases that tell when events happen. Also picture the events in your mind and see if the sequence makes sense.

Read the article about Thurgood Marshall. Look for words and phrases that help you understand the sequence of events in Marshall's life.

Justice Thurgood Marshall

by Lou Ann Walker

In 1908, when Thurgood Marshall was born, most African American and white students in the United States went to separate schools. In many states, African Americans could not vote. Marshall's grandfather had been a slave who was taken from Africa and brought to Maryland. Marshall's father was a waiter on trains and later worked at a club that admitted only white members. All of these things made Marshall question why African Americans were treated differently.

Growing up in Maryland, young Thurgood often got into trouble at school. To punish him, a teacher made him learn parts of the U.S. Constitution. That was excellent training for a student who dreamed of becoming a lawyer. He went to Howard University Law School because the University of Maryland's law school would not accept African Americans. He graduated at the top of his class in 1933.

Thurgood Marshall was a lawyer on many civil rights cases. One of them opened up the University of Maryland to African American students.

His most famous case was in 1954 and was known as *Brown vs. Board of Education*. The case was against the Topeka, Kansas, Board of Education, which had not allowed a black third grader to go to an all-white school near her home. The Supreme Court decided that the segregation, or separation, of black and white students should not be permitted. Marshall had spoken plainly in court, saying, "Equal means getting the same thing, at the same time, and in the same place."

Marshall was appointed to the U.S. Court of Appeals in 1962. Meanwhile, the U.S. Congress was passing important civil rights laws. These laws outlawed discrimination by race. They also helped African Americans in the South to vote as equal citizens.

In 1967, Thurgood Marshall triumphed again. He became the first African American in history to become a U.S. Supreme Court Justice. He served on the Court until 1991.

When Thurgood Marshall died in 1993 at age 84, thousands of people came to bid him farewell. He had shown that the law could help all people to be treated fairly.

Checking Comprehension

1. Why was the court case *Brown vs. Board of Education* so important?

   because African American were treated unfair

2. What inspired young Thurgood Marshall to work for equal rights for African Americans?

   it was right

   _____

Practicing Comprehension Skills

3. Use the selection to complete the time line below. Write a year or an event from Marshall's life on the lines.

1908	Thurgood Marshall is born.
1933	_He graduated at the top of his class_
1954	Wins *Brown vs. Board of Education*
1967	_He became the first African American to become a U.S supreme court Justice._
1991	_He served the court until then._
1993	Thurgood Marshall dies.

4. What was happening in the United States at the same time that Thurgood Marshall became a judge?

   African-American were not being treated equal

Fill in the circle next to the correct answer.

5. Before Thurgood Marshall was appointed to the Court of Appeals, he
   ○ served on the Board of Education.
   ◉ became a justice on the Supreme Court.
   ○ practiced law.
   ○ lived in Kansas.

6. Before *Brown vs. Board of Education,*
   ○ all children had to go to their local school.
   ○ African American children did not go to school.
   ○ only top students could go to school.
   ◉ African American and white children went to separate schools.

Practicing Vocabulary

Choose a word from the box that best matches each definition.
Write the word on the line.

appointed citizens civil Constitution farewell segregation triumphed

_____ 7. goodbye

_____ 8. separation

_____ 9. chosen for an office

_____ 10. members of a nation

_____ 11. describes people's rights

_____ 12. the rules of government for the United States

_____ 13. won, overcame the odds

Writing a Personal Narrative
On a separate sheet of paper, write about a time in your life when you accomplished something that was important to you. Be sure to tell the order of events. Use words and phrases that will help your readers figure out the sequence.

Sequence: Steps in a Process

When you read the **steps in a process,** you can figure out how to do or make something. For example, you use steps in a process when you follow a recipe. Sometimes it's easy to figure out the order of the steps—they are numbered or start with clue words, such as *first, next,* and *finally.* Sometimes you need to use common sense to know the order. It's also helpful to check diagrams or pictures. Then think about what the product looks like at each stage.

Read the steps for making a toy called a *thaumatrope.* As you read, think about the order of the steps.

In the early 1800s, children played with a toy called a *thaumatrope.* To make one, first draw and cut out a cardboard circle. Draw a dog on the circle, then flip it over and draw a doghouse in the same position on the circle. Punch two holes opposite each other a 1/2 inch from the edges.

Insert the end of a rubber band through one hole, making a loop. Next, thread the other end of the rubber band through the loop and pull it tight. Do the same with another rubber band in the other hole.

Hold each rubber band as you turn the circle over and over until the rubber bands are twisted. Finally, pull the bands to make the circle spin quickly. Your brain will see an optical illusion and be tricked into seeing the dog inside the doghouse!

Put the following steps for making a thaumatrope in order. Write the numbers 1 to 5 on the lines.

_____ Loop a rubber band through each hole.

_____ Draw and cut out a circle.

_____ Twist the rubber bands, then pull.

_____ Punch holes on each side of the circle.

_____ Draw a dog on one side and a doghouse on the other side.

> ### Tip
>
> Steps in a process are in a certain order or sequence. Read through all of the steps first before you try to figure out the sequence. Then picture each step in your mind.

As you read the story, think about the sequence of steps the girl follows to make a clay pot.

Coiling the Pot

"My grandmother showed me how to make clay pots," Grandma said, "and now I give this knowledge to you, Marta. Some day, you will show your daughter so that our traditions will not be lost."

Earlier, Grandma and Marta had walked by the goat field on their way to the stream to dig clay. "I first came here for clay 70 years ago," Grandma recalled.

At home, Grandma cut a slab of clay. "First, we make the base," she explained.

Next, Grandma kneaded a handful of clay into a ball. Then Marta too shaped some clay into a ball.

"Roll the ball into an even rope," Grandma instructed. Marta tried, but her clay rope was thick at the ends, while in the middle it was too thin. "Rolling clay takes practice and patience," said Grandma.

"Now we'll place the first coil on the base," Grandma explained. "The ends should meet, so cut away the extra clay."

Once the first coil was in place, Grandma's fingers smoothed the coil down onto the base. She moistened the coil with slip, a mixture of water and clay, while saying, "The first coil is most important."

Marta rolled a second rope of clay and placed it on top of the first. Again Grandma smoothed it while Marta rolled more coils. Soon, the small pot took shape.

"The pot must stand before we trim it," Grandma explained, "so come help me in the garden." Outside, Grandma hoed her squash plants, while Marta picked beans.

Back in the house, the pot was firm, but not hard. Grandma slowly turned the pot. In one hand, she held a trimming tool that she used to carefully trim away the bumps. Soon, the pot was smooth.

"Next, the pot needs to be fired in the oven," Grandma said. "Once it is finished, we can paint it, glaze it, and finally fire it one last time. It's a good thing you'll be here all summer."

Checking Comprehension

1. Why is it important to Grandma that Marta learn to make a coil pot?

_____

_____

2. How can you tell that Grandma lives in the country?

_____

_____

Practicing Comprehension Skills

3. Put these six steps for making a coil clay pot in order. Write the numbers 1 to 6 on the lines.

_____ Add more coils, smoothing each coil onto the one below it.

_____ Place the first coil on the base and cut it to fit.

_____ Cut a slab of clay for the base of the pot.

_____ Press the first coil onto the base and smooth it with slip.

_____ Roll a ball of clay into a rope for the first coil.

_____ Let the pot stand and dry for a while.

Fill in the circle next to the correct answer.

4. After letting the pot stand and dry for a while, what does Grandma do next?

   ○ Trim the pot.

   ○ Paint the pot.

   ○ Coat the pot with slip.

   ○ Fire the pot in the oven.

5. Reread the last paragraph of the story. Write the four steps of making a pot that Marta still has to learn.

First _____

Second _____

Third _____

Fourth _____

Practicing Vocabulary

Write the word from the box that best completes each sentence.

| coil   instructed   kneaded   knowledge   patience   traditions   trim |

6. Each _____ for the pot was a rope of rolled clay.

7. Rolling the clay slowly and carefully takes _____.

8. Step by step, Grandma _____ Marta on how to make the pot.

9. Making pots is one of the _____ that Grandma passed down to Marta.

10. Grandma started to _____ the bumps off the clay pot.

11. With her hands, Marta _____ the clay into a ball.

12. Grandma's _____ of making clay pots came from her grandmother.

Writing a How-To Paragraph
On a separate sheet of paper, tell about something you know how to do. You might describe learning how to hit a baseball, play the guitar, or speak English. As you write, use clue words to show the order of the steps you followed.

Predicting Outcomes

Before you read, you may look at the title and pictures to figure out what a story or an article is about. As you read, you may think about what might happen next. By doing so, you are **making predictions.**

To make a prediction, look for clues that might help you decide what will happen next. Then read on to see if what you predicted actually happens. As you read new information, you may need to change your prediction.

Look at the picture. Predict what the story will be about. As you read, predict how the story might end.

One February morning, Winnie and Cubby saw a poster at the ranger station that read *Montana Wildlife Film Festival.*

"I'd love to be in that festival!" Cubby declared.

"Why not?" Winnie replied. "We're talented!"

Suddenly two strangers stepped out of a car with cameras. Winnie and Cubby lumbered behind the ranger station.

Predict what you think will happen next.

○ The strangers will film wildlife.

○ Winnie and Cubby will take pictures.

Read the rest of the story.

"They've come to take pictures!" snarled Cubby, shaking his big, furry head.

"Let's wrestle!" growled Winnie.

"Get those bears on film!" exclaimed one of the strangers.

When you make a prediction, think about what you have already read. Look for clues in the text and the pictures. Then think about what would make sense.

Was your prediction correct? _____

What clues helped you predict that Winnie and Cubby were bears?

_____

Read the title of the story and look at the picture. Complete the Before Reading section on the chart on page 23 to make a prediction. As you read, look for clues to help you check your prediction.

Diary of a Desperate Contestant

February 15: My video class instructor told us about a contest to film local wildlife. Entries are due March 1. The winner gets to go with a famous filmmaker to Alaska. This will be a cinch!

I'm on my way to fame.

Carlotta

February 17: Today I realized there's little wildlife in a city. I spied two squirrels in a park, but before I could film them, a poodle chased them up an oak tree. I shouted at the poodle, who growled at me.

Later, I convinced my brother Vincent to drive into the countryside. You'd assume I'd find wildlife, but not unless worms, flies, and mosquitoes count!

Help!

Carlotta

February 23: My friend Angela has an uncle who is a farmer. He is always complaining about pesky raccoons, so Angela suggested I tape them for my video.

Today we wandered around the farm. Suddenly I heard Angela gasp, and I turned to see the world's heftiest hog. The hog gave chase, but we were speedier. Once safely over a fence, I filmed the beast snorting at us, but my teacher says a hog is not wildlife.

I'm not ready to give up!

Carlotta

February 28: The deadline nears, and after failing to make my cats act like tiger cubs, I got a desperate idea. I dragged Angela and two pals to a costume shop. By noon, I was filming three ferocious gorillas at play. Vincent even got into the act as an evil gorilla hunter. This may not be what the judges want, but I'm sending it in!

Carlotta

March 15: I won! I didn't get the first prize, but I did receive the "Where There's a Will, There's a Way" award. The judges voted my video the funniest ever. I'm not going to Alaska, but I'm on my way to a career as a filmmaker!

Just say you knew me when.

Carlotta

Checking Comprehension

1. Why is the video contest more difficult than Carlotta thought it would be?

   _____

   _____

2. Why is "Where There's a Will, There's a Way" a good title for the award Carlotta gets for her entry?

   _____

   _____

Practicing Comprehension Skills

3. Look at the chart. Read the prediction you made before reading the story. Now finish the chart. Write what you know happened. Does your prediction match what happened?

BEFORE READING	AFTER READING
What I Predict Will Happen	**What I Know Happened**
Why I Think That Will Happen	**What Might Happen Next**

4. Which two of these story clues could have helped you predict that Carlotta was not going to give up plans for entering the contest? Fill in the circles before the correct answers.

   ○ She had her brother take her to the country to look for wildlife.

   ○ She filmed her friends dressed as gorillas.

   ○ She shouted at the poodle.

   ○ She ran away from the giant hog.

Practicing Vocabulary

Write a word from the box to finish each sentence.

assume cinch deadline desperate heftiest speedier video

5. When everything seemed hopeless, _____ Carlotta came up with a clever plan.

6. To escape to safety, Carlotta had to be _____ than the farmer's hog.

7. The photographer taped a _____ that showed animals in the woods.

8. Carlotta thought filming wild animals would be a _____, but the task was difficult.

9. If you _____ you'll find wildlife in the countryside, you may be disappointed.

10. Judges must receive entries by the March 1 _____.

11. Most hogs are heavy, but the uncle's huge hog was the _____ by far.

MAKING THE
Reading
AND
Writing
CONNECTION

Writing a Journal Entry
Write a new outcome for "Diary of a Desperate Contestant" by writing two journal entries to replace Carlotta's February 28 and March 15 entries. Use a separate sheet of paper.

Recognizing Cause and Effect

While reading a story or an article, you may sometimes stop and think about what happened or why it happened. The reason why something happens is called a **cause**. An **effect** is what happens as the result of a cause. Recognizing causes and effects helps you see how events in a story or details in an article fit together.

Clue words or phrases such as *because, so, since,* or *as a result* may point to a cause or an effect. When there are no clue words, ask yourself, "What happened?" and, "Why did this happen?" An effect may also have more than one cause or a cause may have more than one effect. If no cause is given, decide why something happened from what you read and what you already know.

Read this passage about computers. Think about causes and effects.

Does your home have a computer? If a home has one computer and more than one family member who wants to use it, then the family must share.

Most businesses, especially large ones, provide each employee with a computer. Usually these computers are also shared because they are hooked to a larger, central computer. When computers within a business are connected, workers can share printers and files. They can also send e-mail to each other without having to connect the computer to a telephone line.

> **Tip**
>
> A cause is why something happens. What happens is an effect. Being able to identify causes and effects will help you understand and remember what you read.

Write a cause or an effect from the article to complete the table.

Causes	Effects
A house has one computer.	_____
_____	Workers can share printers and files and send e-mail without a telephone.

Read the story about two sisters and their computers.
Think about what happens and why it happens.

Ask Me a Question

"I installed a new program on the computer in your room," Rachel, my elder sister, announced. She's in high school, but because she is a real computer whiz, local businesses sometimes pay her to help them with their computers.

"Riva, you have to try this program," Rachel added, "because it's totally bliss." Rachel always uses the expression *totally bliss* to describe something she adores.

"Okay, I'll try it," I replied. When I entered my room, I noticed that the computer displayed a new screen saver flashing a message: *Amazing New Program Ready. Just Click Anywhere.*

"Enjoy it," Rachel said, waving from my doorway. I heard the door to her room close as I sat down, moved the cursor, and clicked the mouse.

Ask me a question. I know everything! scrolled across the screen.

I typed swiftly, "What's my name?"

Your name is Riva Borofsky.

I decided that my question was too simple since Rachel could have programmed in some obvious questions and answers. So I came up with something that would not be so easily recognized, and typed, "What color is my shirt?"

The shirt you are currently wearing is red.

I glanced down at my shirt and gasped. How could the computer possibly know? I hurriedly came up with another question: "What are the birthdays of my parents, my sister, and me?"

Father, June 12. Mother, April 5. Rachel, March 10. You, September 22.

"That's absolutely right!" I shrieked.

Before I could type a new question, another message appeared. *March 10 is almost here, what do you contemplate giving your sister?*

I studied the question for a while, then typed, "I'm thinking of giving her some personal services."

Such as?

This was just like having a conversation with a human! I typed hurriedly, "I might do her chores for a couple of weeks."

Totally bliss!

My fingers froze above the keyboard as I stared at the screen. I got up quietly, opened the door to Rachel's room, and saw she was sitting at her computer with a big smile on her face. "I see my 'amazing new program' really works!" she said.

Checking Comprehension

1. What does the narrator discover by the end of the story?

   _____

   _____

2. Why might the author have mentioned at the start that Rachel is a computer whiz?

   _____

   _____

Practicing Comprehension Skills

Complete the chart with causes or effects from the story.

Causes	Effects
3. _____ _____	Riva tries to come up with a harder question.
Using the computer is just like talking to a human.	4. _____ _____ _____
The computer answers questions about Riva's shirt and her family's birthdays.	5. _____ _____ _____

Complete each sentence with a cause or an effect from the story.

6. Rachel is employed by local businesses because

_____

7. Riva's fingers freeze above the keyboard because

_____

_____

8. Riva is thinking of giving Rachel some personal services because

_____

Practicing Vocabulary

Choose the word from the box that best matches each clue. Write the word on the line.

conversation expression installed local personal replied studied

_____ 9. private or individual

_____ 10. answered

_____ 11. chat or talk

_____ 12. learned about

_____ 13. nearby or in the area

_____ 14. words often used together

_____ 15. put a program into a computer

Writing an Informative Paragraph
On another sheet of paper, write a paragraph about a device or machine, such as a computer, that you know how to use. Use words such as *because, so,* and *since* to tell what happens and why.

Using Context Clues

When you come to a word you do not know while reading, what do you do? You can look up the word in a glossary or dictionary. You can also read words, sentences, or paragraphs around the unknown word to find clues that may help you figure out the meaning. The clues that you get from the words, sentences, or paragraphs around the unknown word are called **context clues.**

Look for context clues to help you with the meaning of the word *terrain* in the following sentence.

The Mars terrain includes craters, canyons, volcanoes, and flat plains.

The words *craters, canyons, volcanoes,* and *flat plains* are all landforms. Using these context clues, you can guess that *terrain* means "an area of land and its features."

Read the following article. Use context clues to figure out the meaning of the underlined word.

Where do you think the largest known volcano is? It's on Mars. Olympus Mons is the largest volcano known in the solar system. It is more than twice as tall as Mauna Loa in Hawaii, which is the largest volcano on Earth. Olympus Mons measures about 15 miles from its base up to its <u>summit</u>.

Look for context clues in the article that help you understand the meaning of the underlined word. Write the clues on the lines below.

_____

_____

What does the word *summit* mean? _____

Tip

Look for different kinds of context clues. Ask yourself, "Does the sentence have a synonym for the unknown word? Does the sentence give a definition of the word?"

On Your Own

Read the article about Mars. As you read, think about the underlined words. Look for context clues that will help you understand these words.

Mission to Mars

For hundreds of years, people have gazed upward at Mars in the night sky and wondered, "What is it like up there? Does anyone live there?" They had to wait to actually investigate the planet until 1965 when a spacecraft, *Mariner 4*, landed on Mars. Several other probes followed. A lander named *Pathfinder* finally was launched toward Mars on December 4, 1996. This mission to Mars told people a lot about the planet nearest Earth in the solar system.

Pathfinder landed on Mars on July 4, 1997. Airbags helped soften the impact of the landing so that the craft would not be damaged. Then a door in *Pathfinder* opened and out came *Sojourner*, a six-wheeled robot rover designed to take pictures and collect information. *Sojourner* traveled over the surface of Mars collecting information about the planet's rocks and soil. Scientists on Earth controlled the movements of *Sojourner* as it explored the Martian terrain.

The *Pathfinder* mission was a great success. The spacecraft itself operated three times longer than scientists had expected. The rover worked twelve times longer. *Sojourner* sent 2.6 billion bits of information back to Earth, including more than 16,000 images, or pictures. Here are some of the things *Pathfinder* helped scientists learn:

- It is probable that there is sand on Mars.
- The atmosphere of Mars has clouds.
- Floods may have once ravaged the planet's surface.
- Temperatures fluctuate from extreme hot to cold.

Exploring Mars may reveal whether there could be life anywhere else in the universe. Information about the climate on Mars can help people understand climatic changes on Earth. Scientists also harbor hopes to terraform Mars, which would make it possible for humans to live there. The United States is looking toward the future by planning more missions to Mars.

Checking Comprehension

1. What is the difference between a lander and a rover?

   _____

   _____

2. How did *Sojourner* help make the *Pathfinder* mission a success?

   _____

   _____

Practicing Comprehension Skills

Read the choices for the meaning of each word. Go back to the article and look for context clues. Fill in the circle next to the correct meaning.

3. The word *probes* means _____

   ○ exploration machines   ○ tape recorders   ○ digital cameras   ○ test tubes

4. What words in the story gave you a clue to the meaning of *probe*?

   _____

5. The word *impact* means _____

   ○ rocket launch   ○ flat surface   ○ a crash   ○ orbiting planet

6. What words in the story gave you a clue to the meaning of *impact*?

   _____

   _____

7. The word *terraform* means _____

   ○ make possible for humans   ○ spend more time and money
     to live somewhere   making Earth livable

   ○ explore the solar system   ○ find information about life
     with astronauts   elsewhere in the universe

Look at the article again. Find the meaning of each word listed below.
Write the meaning and the context clues that helped you.

Word	Meaning	Context Clues
8. rover	_____	_____
		_____
9. terrain	_____	_____
10. fluctuate	_____	_____

Practicing Vocabulary

Write the word from the box that replaces the underlined word or words.

climatic   extreme   harbor   investigate   ravaged   robot   spacecraft

_____ 11. *Pathfinder* helped scientists <u>examine</u> Mars.

_____ 12. A <u>machine</u> takes pictures of the rocks on Mars.

_____ 13. <u>Weather</u> changes on Mars include high and low temperatures.

_____ 14. A crowd watched the launch of the <u>machine used for space flight</u>.

_____ 15. People could not survive the <u>great</u> temperatures on Mars.

_____ 16. Scientists <u>have</u> hopes that people can live on Mars.

_____ 17. Floods <u>caused great damage to</u> the planet's landscape.

Writing a Report
Work with a partner and imagine that you are moving to Mars.
On another sheet of paper, write about what you would take
with you and why. Include context clues for difficult words.

Comparing and Contrasting

When you look at two things to see how they are alike or different, you **are comparing** and **contrasting** them. A comparison tells how two or more things are alike. A contrast tells how two or more things are different. Clue words such as *like, same, both,* and *as* can signal comparisons. Clue words such as *different, however, unlike,* and *but* can signal contrasts.

Identifying how things are alike and how they are different can help you notice details and add to your understanding. Writers do not always use clue words or compare and contrast things for you, so it is important to know how to do so on your own.

Read the following article. Look for comparisons and contrasts.

How did Native Americans travel long ago? The answer depends on where the people lived.

There were many forests and rivers in the Northeast. The Iroquois of the coastal regions made watertight canoes by stretching elm or birch bark over wooden frames.

The Northwest also had forests and rivers. The Haida people used tools to hollow out logs to make boats. These were called dugout canoes.

Write a comparison between the Northeast and the Northwest.

_____

_____

Fill in the circle next to the sentence that shows a contrast between Iroquois and Haida canoes.

○ The Iroquois stretched bark over a frame, while the Haida hollowed out logs.

○ Both the Iroquois and the Haida used trees to make canoes.

Tip

You can use comparing and contrasting to explain something unfamiliar. Show how it is like and unlike something that is familiar.

STRATEGY: Comparing and Contrasting   33

As you read about how different Native Americans built homes, pay attention to how the author uses comparisons and contrasts to help you understand. Look for clue words to help you.

The Longhouse and the Tipi

by Joseph Bruchac

In the old days, wherever Native American people lived, their homes reflected their way of life. The traditional houses of the Iroquois of the northeastern woodlands are very different from the dwellings of the Lakhotas of the Great Plains.

The Iroquois called themselves Haudenosaunee (how-dee-no-SHO-nee), "People of the Longhouse." Their homes were long buildings made of wooden poles sunk into the earth, lashed together, and covered with overlapping shingles made of pieces of elm bark. In contrast, the Lakhotas lived in homes made of buffalo skins fastened around a cone-shaped frame of tall poles tied together. These skin lodges were called tipis (TEE-peez).

Each Iroquois longhouse held a number of families, who shared the cooking fires in the center. Some longhouses were very large, up to 200 feet long and 40 feet wide. A Lakhota tipi, however, was built to house a single tiyospaye (tee-YO-shpay), or extended family. The average tipi was about 20 feet in diameter with 25-foot-high tipi poles.

Longhouse villages were built close to rivers, where the soil was good for farming. Stockades were sometimes built around these villages to protect them from enemies. Because the Iroquois relied both on hunting and on the corn, beans, and squash their gardens yielded, their villages would remain in one place for a decade or more. When game became scarce or the soil was no longer fertile, they would construct a new village in another location.

The Lakhotas relied mainly on shifting herds of buffalo for their food, so their houses had to be easily movable. An entire tipi village could be set up or taken down in a matter of hours. Tipi poles would be fastened to either side of a horse to make a travois (trah-VWAH) that could be used to drag away their possessions. The Lakhota did not plant gardens as the Iroquois did.

Fruits and edible roots were gathered by Lakhota women, while the men hunted game animals for food.

As different as they were, the homes of both the Iroquois and the Lakhota demonstrate how each of these native peoples adapted to the natural world.

Checking Comprehension

1. Why did the Iroquois and the Lakhota set up homes in new places?

    _____

    _____

2. How did the materials used to build a home reflect where the Iroquois and the Lakhota lived?

    _____

    _____

Practicing Comprehension Skills

Read each question. Fill in the circle next to the best answer.

3. How were the traditional ways of the Iroquois and Lakhota alike?

    ○ Both hunted for food.   ○ Both lived in wooden houses.

    ○ Both planted gardens.   ○ Both depended on the buffalo.

4. Which is a difference between the Iroquois and Lakhota?

    ○ The Lakhota lived in family groups, but the Iroquois did not.

    ○ The Iroquois gathered and ate fruits, but the Lakhota did not.

    ○ The Iroquois stayed in one place, while the Lakhota moved around.

    ○ The Lakhota lived in longhouses, but the Iroquois lived in tipis.

5. Longhouses were built near _____

    ○ plains   ○ rivers   ○ buffalo herds   ○ stockades

6. Tipis were set up near _____

    ○ gardens   ○ stockades   ○ rivers   ○ buffalo herds

Complete the chart. Write contrasting details from the article in each column.

	Iroquois Longhouses	Lakhota Tipis
How were their homes built?	7. _____ _____ _____	8. _____ _____ _____
How big were their homes?	9. _____ _____ _____	10. _____ _____ _____

Practicing Vocabulary

Choose the word from the box that best matches each definition.
Write the word on the line.

demonstrate diameter pieces possessions reflected stockades yielded

_____ 11. belongings

_____ 12. bits or parts

_____ 13. show or prove

_____ 14. fences or walls

_____ 15. produced

_____ 16. width of a circle

_____ 17. formed a picture of

MAKING THE Reading AND Writing CONNECTION

Writing a Compare and Contrast Paragraph
On another sheet of paper, write a paragraph about two people, two things, or two places you know or have read about. Tell how they are alike and how they are different.

Summarizing

A good way to remember a story or an article is to think about the most important ideas after you finish reading and write a **summary**. A summary is a short statement in your own words that tells about the main ideas of an article or the most important parts of a story. A summary for an article should tell the main ideas and leave out unimportant details. Ask yourself who, what, when, and where to help you find the main ideas. A summary for a story should tell the important parts, such as the goals of the characters, how they tried to reach these goals, and whether they succeeded.

Read this article. Think about which ideas are the most important and should appear in a summary.

Quick! Name the king of the dinosaurs. If you answered Tyrannosaurus rex, you're right.

An adult T. rex male weighed in at about 10,000 pounds. It was almost 30 feet tall as well. Even though it was big, the T. rex could run about 30 miles an hour. As a result, it could quickly overtake its prey and use sharp teeth as long as bananas to chew through flesh and bone. Small animals were T. rex's favorite meal.

Tyrannosaurus rex means "tyrant lizard king." Do you think this is a good name for this huge dinosaur?

Decide which summary is best. Explain your choice on the lines.

A. Tyrannosaurus rex had sharp teeth that it used to eat meat. Its teeth were as big as bananas. It was also big and fast.

B. Tyrannosaurus rex was the king of the dinosaurs. It was big and tall, with long, sharp teeth. It could run fast to catch smaller animals. Its name means "tyrant lizard king."

_____

_____

Tip

A good summary lists only the most important ideas of a story or article. You can use a summary to help you remember the main points in what you have read.

Read this article about ancient animals. As you read, think about which ideas you would include in a summary.

Giants of the Air and Sea

by J. Lynett Gillette

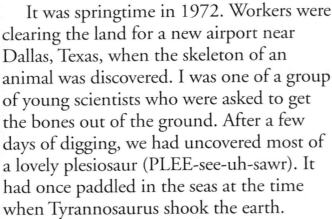

It was springtime in 1972. Workers were clearing the land for a new airport near Dallas, Texas, when the skeleton of an animal was discovered. I was one of a group of young scientists who were asked to get the bones out of the ground. After a few days of digging, we had uncovered most of a lovely plesiosaur (PLEE-see-uh-sawr). It had once paddled in the seas at the time when Tyrannosaurus shook the earth.

Not everyone had heard of plesiosaurs, so we tried to describe this 30-foot-long swimming lizard to the reporter who visited the site. The next day, the newspaper announced that we had discovered a giant fossil bat! If it had been a bat, it would indeed have been a giant. It was a lesson for me. Animals that don't live today are hard to imagine.

The first people to uncover pterodactyls (ter-uh-DACK-tilz) had a similar problem. Bones of these creatures had been seen for a long time in England and Germany. No one was sure which group of animals were their relatives. Some described the creatures as having the arms of a vampire bat, the teeth of a crocodile, the vertebrae of a lizard, and the beak of a bird.

What do you get when you put all those things together? Paleontologists, scientists who study ancient life, pooled all the evidence, and finally agreed that the fossils were flying reptiles. The fossils had a long fourth finger on each hand. Skin had stretched between this finger and the hind legs. That allowed the pterodactyls to glide and swoop down on prey and perhaps flap a little to get back up to a perch. Clearly the pterodactyl was not a bat and not a bird. It was just another kind of reptile, one that took to the skies. Some pterodactyls grew enormous, up to 40 feet in length.

Dinosaurs walked, but plesiosaurs swam and pterodactyls flew or glided. Each of the three types of reptiles lived in the ancient world. Today, there are no living reptile giants to match them.

Checking Comprehension

1. If you found a plesiosaur skeleton, what might it tell you about the area?

   _____

   _____

2. How are plesiosaurs and pterodactyls alike and different?

   _____

   _____

Practicing Comprehension Skills

Read the details from "Giants of the Air and Sea." Write a summary sentence that tells the most important idea or ideas.

3. Workers were clearing the land for a new airport near Dallas. After a few days of digging, we had uncovered most of a lovely plesiosaur.

   _____

4. Some described pterodactyls as having the arms of a vampire bat, the teeth of a crocodile, the vertebrae of a lizard, and the beak of a bird. Scientists finally agreed that the fossils were flying reptiles.

   _____

5. Clearly the pterodactyl was not a bat and not a bird. It was just another kind of reptile, one that took to the skies. Some pterodactyls grew enormous, up to 40 feet in length.

   _____

6. Not everyone had heard of plesiosaurs, so we tried to describe this 30-foot-long swimming lizard to the reporter who visited the site.

   _____

7. Write a summary of "Giants of the Air and Sea."

_____

_____

_____

_____

_____

Practicing Vocabulary

Choose a word from the box that best replaces the underlined word
or words. Write the word on the line.

ancient describe evidence pooled relatives reptiles swoop

_____ 8. Lizards are <u>cold-blooded animals with scales</u>.

_____ 9. Dinosaurs are creatures of <u>prehistoric</u> times.

_____ 10. Different kinds of reptiles are <u>animals in the same family</u>.

_____ 11. Scientists look at all the <u>proof and facts</u> before drawing a
conclusion.

_____ 12. Flying creatures <u>make sweeping moves</u> down from cliffs.

_____ 13. Can you <u>tell about</u> strange animals of the past?

_____ 14. Scientists <u>put together</u> all of their information about
reptiles that lived long ago.

Writing a Summary
What is your typical day at school like? On another sheet of
paper, write a summary of your activities. Don't tell everything!
Tell only the most important things you usually do.

Paraphrasing

How would you share an article or story you have read? You would probably tell the information in your own words. When you explain or retell something in your own words, you are **paraphrasing.** There are many ways to say the same thing. Read the following two sentences.

There was a very small river flowing through the canyon.

A small stream ran through the canyon.

The second sentence is a paraphrase of the first sentence. A good paraphrase uses different words but still includes all of the author's ideas. Paraphrasing helps you remember what you read and check if you understood an article or story.

Read Jerry's diary. Think about how you might paraphrase what Jerry wrote.

Dear Diary,

I wasn't thrilled when Dad handed me the brochure. On the front a headline said, "Bike Down the World's Largest Dormant Volcano!" Inside was a description of a bike trip up and down Mt. Haleakala in Hawaii.

I was nervous as Dad and I reached the summit at 10,000 feet and started down the other side. You might think biking down a mountain is a breeze, but it's very frightening. I'm glad I did it, but I'm not so sure I want to go again.

Jerry

Think about the information you just read. Fill in the circle next to the paraphrase that has the same meaning.

○ Jerry wasn't sure he wanted to go on a bike trip on Mt. Haleakala in Hawaii. Once he reached the top, he was scared about going down. He's glad he went, but he's not sure he'd go again.

○ Jerry didn't want to go on a bike trip to Mt. Haleakala, which is a volcano in Hawaii. He didn't like what he read about it. He worried all the way to the top. Then he was scared to go down.

> ## Tip
>
> When you paraphrase, or retell, an article or story, ask yourself, "Did I include all of the author's ideas? Did I use my own words?"

Read the article about mountain bikes. Think about how you would paraphrase sentences.

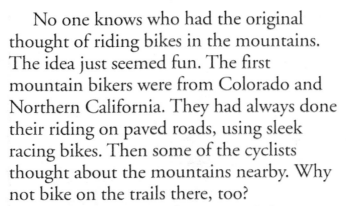
A Hike on a Bike

by Marian Calabro

No one knows who had the original thought of riding bikes in the mountains. The idea just seemed fun. The first mountain bikers were from Colorado and Northern California. They had always done their riding on paved roads, using sleek racing bikes. Then some of the cyclists thought about the mountains nearby. Why not bike on the trails there, too?

The problem was that racing bikes weren't tough enough. For off-road riding, you need a sturdier bike. It has to have wide tires to grip dirt roads, and high clearance between the frame and the ground. Stores didn't sell that kind of bike then, so the cyclists devised their own. Searching through garages and junkyards, the cyclists found old "clunker" bikes that had once been popular. They cleaned the rusted frames, added strong handlebars, and put on heavy-duty tires.

Cyclists in different areas heard about mountain biking, and the movement spread. Soon the mountain bikers were teaching themselves tricky moves, such as jumping their bikes over rocks and logs.

In a short time, mountain bikers raced each other down steep trails and mountain passes. Sometimes they took it easy and just enjoyed the views—as if they were doing a hike on a bike. To prevent injuries, mountain bikers, like other bicyclists, began wearing helmets and other safety equipment.

One winter, with no snow for skiing, mountain bikers in Crested Butte, Colorado, held a "Fat Tire Festival!" Bicycle manufacturers spotted the sport as a growing trend. Almost as soon as the companies began mass-producing them, mountain bikes became America's best-selling type of bike. They're comfortable and fun to ride, even if you never ride them off-road, away from paved paths.

Today, a quick search on the World Wide Web turns up mountain biking clubs worldwide. Mountain bike racing has been added to the Olympic Summer Games. The sport is so popular that it has its own Hall of Fame and Museum—located in Crested Butte, of course.

Checking Comprehension

1. How are mountain bikes different from racing bikes?

   _____

   _____

2. What are some things mountain bikers do?

   _____

   _____

Practicing Comprehension Skills

Read the following sentence from "A Hike on a Bike." Fill in the circle next to the best paraphrase.

3. Stores didn't sell that kind of bike then, so the cyclists devised their own.

   ○ Bike riders made mountain bikes to sell in stores.

   ○ Cyclists could not buy mountain bikes.

   ○ Racing bikes could not be used on mountain trails.

   ○ Bike riders made their own mountain bikes then because they couldn't buy them in stores.

Paraphrase the following sentences from "A Hike on a Bike."

4. No one knows who had the original idea of riding bikes in the mountains.

   _____

   _____

5. To prevent injuries, mountain bikers, like other bicyclists, began wearing helmets and other safety equipment.

   _____

   _____

6. Choose the best paraphrase of the last paragraph of the article.

○ On the World Wide Web, you'll see mountain biking clubs. Bike racing is in the Summer Olympics and in a museum.

○ The World Wide Web lists mountain biking clubs worldwide. Mountain bike racing is in the Olympic Summer Games. The sport has its own Hall of Fame and Museum.

○ The World Wide Web features mountain biking clubs from around the world. Mountain bike racing is new to the Summer Olympics. A Hall of Fame and Museum opened in Crested Butte.

○ There are mountain biking clubs all over the world. Bike racing now has its own Hall of Fame and Museum.

Practicing Vocabulary

Write a word from the box to replace each underlined word or words.

clearance	comfortable	cyclists	injuries	passes	sturdier	trend

_____ 7. <u>Bicycle riders</u> first made mountain bikes out of old parts.

_____ 8. Falling off a bike sometimes causes <u>cuts and scrapes</u>.

_____ 9. Moutain <u>roads</u> can be steep and narrow.

_____ 10. Padded seats make bike riding more <u>enjoyable</u>.

_____ 11. Wide tires make bikes <u>stronger</u>.

_____ 12. <u>Space</u> between the bike and ground makes bikes safer.

_____ 13. Mountain biking is the <u>direction</u> in bicycling today.

Writing a Personal Narrative
On a separate sheet of paper, write a paragraph about a sport or hobby, such as bike racing, that interests you. Then exchange papers with a partner. Write a paraphrase of each other's work.

Author's Purpose

What reasons do authors have for writing? An author might write to entertain readers with stories or to explain information. An author also may write to express feelings or to persuade readers to think in certain ways.

The reason an author has for writing is called the **author's purpose.** In many stories and articles an author has more than one purpose for writing, such as to entertain and to inform. Understanding an author's purpose can help you decide how to read a piece of writing. You may want to read quickly if a piece is written to entertain, or read slowly if a piece is written to give you information.

Read the article from a school newspaper. Think about the author's purpose for writing.

My Violin by Steve Diaz

I have been taking violin lessons for two years, and I think it's the best instrument to play. The violin is the most interesting musical instrument because it can make so many different sounds.

When I play the violin, I feel like I am hovering inside a cloud, and an hour feels as though it's only a minute. In my opinion, more kids should learn to play this great musical instrument.

What were Steve's purposes for writing this article? Write **Yes** or **No** on the line next to each purpose.

_____ to inform people about how violins are made

_____ to express his feelings about playing the violin

_____ to entertain readers with a good story

_____ to persuade readers to learn how to play the violin

Tip

Before you read an article or story, look at the title and pictures. They may give clues to the author's purpose for writing. Then you can adjust how quickly or slowly you read.

Read the title of the article. Look at the pictures. What do you think the article will be about? Why do you think the author might have written it? As you read, think about the author's purposes.

Midori Helps Others While Making Music

At the Tanglewood Music Festival in Massachusetts, the violinist played so energetically that she broke a string on her instrument. Then she borrowed a violin from an orchestra member who was accompanying her. Amazingly, she broke a string on that violin, too. She calmly completed the concert using a third violin. Is this an unusual story? Yes, and what is even more incredible is that the violinist was a 14-year-old girl named Midori.

When Midori was just three years old, her mother, a professional violinist in Japan, gave her lessons on a tiny violin one-sixteenth the size of a regular instrument. Right from the start Midori played smoothly with no awkward movements. Her awesome talent was obvious. When she was 10 years old, the great conductor Zubin Mehta heard her play. He was so impressed that he invited her to perform at the New York Philharmonic orchestra's New Year's Eve concert. The whole audience stood to applaud and cheer her, and her professional career began.

As she grew older, Midori lost interest in the violin. She left music school, and she began to cancel concerts. Perhaps she had been pursuing her dream too hard for too long and she just needed some time to be a normal teenager.

When she was 21, Midori founded Midori and Friends, an organization whose goal is to bring classical music into New York City's public schools. She performed at every participating school and even began to play for children in hospitals. "I love working with children," she remarked. "I see their eyes sparkle, even when they're very sick. When they listen to the music and they respond, it's a great experience."

Now Midori is back performing and recording. Critics say that her playing is even more wonderful. She has found that helping others can make her music better than ever.

Checking Comprehension

1. How would you summarize the major events in Midori's career?

    _____

    _____

    _____

2. How is Midori's work with children like performing in a concert?
    How is it different?

    _____

    _____

    _____

Practicing Comprehension Skills

3. Put a check mark next to a statement that is true about "Midori
    Helps Others While Making Music."

    _____ The author wrote mainly to persuade people to play the violin.

    _____ The author was writing to inform readers about Midori's life and career.

    _____ The author wrote mainly to explain how to play the violin.

    _____ The author's purpose was to express feelings about playing the violin.

4. Explain how you figured out the answer to question 3.

    _____

    _____

5. How did the title of the article and the pictures help you figure
    out the author's purpose?

    _____

    _____

6. Reread the first paragraph of the article. What other purpose do you think the author might have had for writing? How do you know?

_____

_____

Fill in the circle next to the correct answer.

7. If the author wanted to entertain readers, which two of the following might he or she write?

○ a play about a violin player   ○ a review of one of Midori's concerts

○ a description of a violin   ○ a story about a lonely violin

Practicing Vocabulary

Write a word from the box to finish each sentence.

accompanying applaud awkward critics instrument orchestra talent

8. The violinist came out on stage carrying her _____.

9. She was followed by a pianist who would be _____ her.

10. Tonight they would also play with a famous _____.

11. The violinist's _____ had impressed the conductor.

12. When the _____ heard the concert, they were also impressed.

13. There was an _____ moment when she dropped her bow.

14. She must have been excited when she heard the audience _____.

MAKING THE Reading AND Writing CONNECTION

Writing a Paragraph
On a separate sheet of paper, write a paragraph about a musical performer you like. First, decide whether your purpose will be to give information, express feelings, persuade, or entertain.

Statements of Fact and Opinion

What is the difference between a fact and an opinion? A **statement of fact** can be proved true or false. A **statement of opinion** cannot be proved true or false because it tells someone's ideas, feelings, or beliefs. Writers may identify opinions with phrases such as *I think, I feel, I believe,* and *in my opinion*. Comparative words such as *best* and *worst* and descriptive words such as *pretty* and *funny* may also point to an opinion. Read the following sentences:

Fact: Roller skates were invented in 1760.

Opinion: Roller-skating is the best way to exercise.

You could prove the first statement true or false by reading about roller skates or by asking an expert on roller-skating. No one can prove that roller-skating is the best way to exercise. That is just the way the writer feels.

Read about the history of roller skates. As you read, look for statements of fact and statements of opinion.

We should thank Joseph Merlin for inventing roller skates. The Belgian inventor created the first pair in 1760. These skates had small metal wheels that attached to a shoe. In 1819 a French inventor named Petitbled made wooden skates with wheels set in a straight line. On these, skaters could only go in a straight line. That must have been boring! James Plimpton of Massachusetts made a pair of "rocking skates" in 1863. The four wheels were set in a rectangle and worked on rubber springs, so people could skate in curves.

On the line next to each statement, write the letter **F** for **fact** or the letter **O** for **opinion.**

_____ We should thank Joseph Merlin for roller skates.

_____ In 1819, Petitbled made wooden skates.

_____ That must have been boring!

Tip

A statement of opinion may sound like a fact because it seems to be true or it contains a fact as well as an opinion. People can have different opinions, but facts don't change.

As you read about in-line skating, look for statements of fact and statements of opinion.

Get In-Line!

You should join the nearly 25 million people around the world who are in-line skaters. In-line skating is faster and smoother than regular roller-skating. Some people say that it feels like ice-skating without the ice or like running on wheels.

A regular roller skate has four wheels arranged in a rectangle, but the wheels on an in-line skate are arranged in a straight line. When you turn a corner on a regular skate, the inner wheels travel a shorter distance than the outer wheels. Turns make you wobble and slow down. When you turn on in-line skates, however, you glide easily because all the wheels travel the same distance. That's why regular roller-skating is boring and in-line skating is exciting.

There are different kinds of in-line skating. Beginning skaters usually skate for fun. This is called recreational, or "rec" skating. More experienced skaters may play roller hockey or race. "Aggressive skating," in which skaters make fancy jumps, or "airs," using ramps, is the most awesome. Aggressive skaters

gather for competitions that are amazing to watch.

Before you try in-line skating, you need some basic equipment. First, you need to buy or rent your skates. Make sure that they are comfortable, not too tight and not too loose. Skates that fit correctly support your feet. Then protect other parts of your body with a helmet, elbow pads, wrist guards, and knee pads. Always remember that pavement is hard, and your body is soft!

Once you are padded in all the important places, you're ready to start. One good way to begin learning to use in-line skates is to "duck walk" on grass or a thick carpet. When you duck walk, you point your skates outward in a V-shape.

After you've practiced walking, you can try stroking and gliding on a hard, smooth surface. In no time, you'll be whizzing along a path.

So go ahead, get in-line! Though you better watch out—you may become a loyal in-line skater. There's nothing more exhilarating than speeding through a park on a sunny day.

Checking Comprehension

1. Why do so many people who try in-line skating become loyal skaters?

   _____

2. How are recreational skating and aggressive skating different?

   _____

   _____

Practicing Comprehension Skills

Read the following sentences. Write **F** next to each statement of fact and **O** next to each statement of opinion.

3. _____ In-line skating is smoother than regular roller-skating.

4. _____ A regular roller skate has four wheels arranged in a rectangle.

5. _____ That's why regular roller-skating is boring and in-line skating is exciting.

6. _____ There are different kinds of in-line skating.

7. _____ The most awesome kind of in-line skating is called "aggressive skating."

8. _____ Aggressive skaters do fancy jumps, or "airs," using ramps.

9. _____ Before you try in-line skating, you need some basic equipment.

10. _____ There's nothing more exhilarating than speeding through a park.

Read the following sentences from the article. They contain both facts and opinions. In each sentence, underline the part that states a fact. Circle the part that states an opinion.

11. You should join the nearly 25 million people around the world who are in-line skaters.

12. Aggressive skaters gather for competitions that are amazing to watch.

Read the chart. Rewrite the fact as an opinion. Rewrite the opinion as a fact.

Fact	Opinion
13. _____ _____ _____	The best way to begin is to "duck walk" on grass or a thick carpet.
When you turn on in-line skates, you glide easily because all the wheels travel the same distance.	14. _____ _____ _____

Practicing Vocabulary

Write the word from the box that belongs in each group.

exhilarating   join   loyal   protect   recreational   rectangle   wobble

15. triangle, circle, _____

16. become part of, unite, _____

17. for fun, for pleasure, _____

18. guard, defend, _____

19. exciting, fun, _____

20. shake, roll back and forth, _____

21. dedicated, faithful, _____

Writing a Persuasive Paragraph
On a separate sheet of paper, write a paragraph about a game or sport you enjoy. Try to persuade your readers to try the activity. Include statements of fact and statements of opinion.

Making Judgments

When you are reading a story, do you ever stop to think about how you feel about the characters? You may have thought that a character acted in the right way or made a bad decision. Have you ever felt as if an author was trying to shape your opinions? You may have decided that you agreed or did not agree with what the author wrote.

When you form an opinion about a character or event, or about what an author wrote about a subject, you are **making a judgment.** Making judgments means thinking about and deciding how you feel about people, situations, and issues you read. Use your own experiences and values, along with careful reading to make judgments. Then look for evidence in your reading to support your judgments.

Read this letter from a story character. As you read, make judgments about the character.

Sacramento, California
April 1860

Dearest Mother,

You hold a letter that I had a minor part in delivering, for I am now one of the Pony Express messengers who carries mail from here to St. Joseph, Missouri. The advertisements for riders asked for brave and adventurous young men such as myself, so I applied without any hesitation.

I have galloped through mud that nearly trapped my trusty horse and fought my way through a mountain snowstorm. It is an important task, and I am excited to be doing it. I shall not say more, for I know you fret about my safety.

Your loving son,
Ezra

Do you think it was a good idea for Ezra to go to work for the Pony Express? Why or why not?

_____

_____

> ## Tip
>
> After you have made a judgment, test if your judgment is correct. Look for evidence in the story or article to support your opinion.

On Your Own

Read this story about an American family in the early 1850s. Make judgments based on what you read.

Starting Out on the Oregon Trail

After Annabeth's father had caught "Oregon fever," he never ceased talking about the fertile land of the Willamette Valley. Although Annabeth was also eager to see new places and meet fresh faces, Mama did not share their enthusiasm. "I won't leave Missouri," Mama declared gruffly. "I am happy here."

Father continued to argue. "Just listen to this letter from Uncle Paul. He and his family made the journey without many problems, and he describes how amazing the land is."

Mama listened and then replied, "Oregon country may be beautiful, but it is 2,000 miles away, and there are several dangers along the trail."

Father persisted until finally Mama agreed, saying, "If you must see Oregon, we will accompany you." Annabeth tried to stay quietly in bed, but she was so excited that she tumbled to the floor.

After weeks of preparations, Father, Mama, Annabeth, and baby James waited on the shore of the Missouri River. When the ferryman hailed them, Father coaxed the oxen onto the ferry, and the wagon and its cargo began the crossing.

"The ferry has water in it!" Annabeth suddenly announced. The oxen had moved, causing one side of the ferry to dip lower, and water was pouring over the edge. Soon the ferry was entirely underwater, and the wagon was slowly sinking. "I'll get a boat," said the ferryman before diving into the swirling water.

Mama clutched the top of a wagon wheel as the water rose, while Father sat on the wagon seat, holding James. Annabeth climbed into the wagon and stood on a trunk. The water quickly reached her knees, and then rose up to her shoulders. Could she pull herself higher?

Then Annabeth heard Mama's terrified voice, crying, "Where is Annabeth?"

"Here I am," chirped Annabeth, peering out to see Mama, Father, and James sitting in the ferryman's little boat. She climbed down to join them. As he rowed the soaked, chilled passengers to shore, the ferryman assured the family, "Don't worry, I'll get your wagon across. This has happened before."

Annabeth decided she was looking forward to further adventures on the journey ahead.

Checking Comprehension

1. What is a main difference between Annabeth's mother and father?

   _____

   _____

2. How does Annabeth feel about the journey? How can you tell?

   _____

   _____

Practicing Comprehension Skills

3. Which of the following judgments can you make about Annabeth?

   ○ Annabeth seems daring and bold.   ○ Annabeth argues too much.

   ○ Annabeth is easily bored.   ○ Annabeth should speak up more.

4. Write three reasons from the story to support the judgment you chose in item 3.

   _____

   _____

   _____

5. Do you think the family should continue their journey? Give reasons for your answer. Use evidence from the story, your own experiences, and your understanding of the story.

   _____

   _____

   _____

6. Fill in the circle before the word that best describes Mama.

   ○ adventurous   ○ shy   ○ cautious   ○ curious

7. Use the graphic organizer to show proof from the story that supports your answer to item 6. Write your answer to item 6 in the top box. In each of the boxes below, write one event from the story that supports your answer.

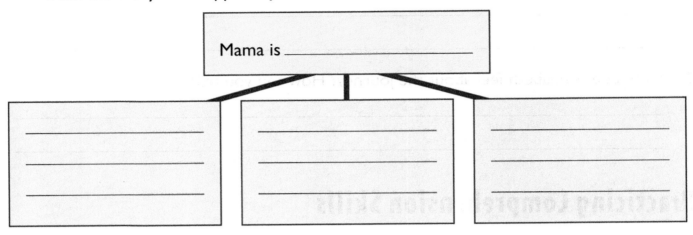

Mama is _____

Practicing Vocabulary

Choose a word from the box that best completes each analogy.

announced	assured	cargo	coaxed	eager	fertile	persisted

8. *Productive* is to _____ as *barren* is to *unproductive.*

9. *Happy* is to *sad* as *disinterested* is to _____.

10. *Soothed* is to *calmed* as *persuaded* is to _____.

11. *Written* is to *recorded* as *reported* is to _____.

12. *Determined* is to _____ as *messy* is to *sloppy.*

13. *Freight* is to *train* as _____ is to *ship.*

14. *Encouraged* is to _____ as *despaired* is to *discouraged.*

Writing an Adventure Story
Think about one of your favorite story characters. On another sheet of paper, write the beginning of your own story about an adventure that this character might have. Include clues that will help readers make judgments about the character.

Point of View

When you begin to read a story, one of the first things you find out is who is telling the story. An author can choose to tell a story in different ways.

In some stories, a character tells the story using words like *I*, *me*, and *we* to tell about events and his or her feelings and thoughts. The reader experiences the story along with the character. This is called **first-person point of view**.

Example: *I* **worried when** *we* **jumped into the ice-cold pool.**

In the **third-person point of view**, someone outside of the story, called the *narrator*, tells what happens. The narrator uses words like *he, she, it*, and *they* to tell readers what all of the characters are thinking and feeling.

Example: *Melanie* **couldn't wait to jump into the ice-cold pool, but** *Rob* **was a little worried.**

Knowing the point of view will help you follow and understand a story.

Read this story beginning. Think about the point of view, or who is telling the story.

Jeff shivered in the shallow water, partly from cold but mostly from terror. He stared at the raft in the middle of the small lake where two of his friends were relaxing. They looked so far away!

"Just pivot your arms, kick your legs, and always breathe evenly," said Lamont, "and you'll get to the raft faster than you think." Jeff's swimming instructor knew what it was like to swim to the raft for the first time.

Jeff was in the beginning swimming group with the youngest kids. That was embarrassing. Now, if he passed this swimming test, he would be able to swim in deeper water.

What is the point of view of the story? How do you know?

_____

_____

_____

> **Tip**
>
> To think about point of view, ask yourself, "Is a character or an outside narrator telling the story?" and "How would the story be different from another point of view?"

Read each story about a girl's experiences at summer camp. As you read, decide what the point of view is.

Star Struck!

Felice was spending the summer at camp, and at first, she felt lonely. All the girls in her cabin had been to Camp Wildfern before, but this was Felice's first time. The other campers' excitement made her feel even more alone.

At the end of her first week, Felice became pals with Teri. The girls liked each other and shared many interests.

One morning, a poster attracted their attention. It said, "Audition for the Camp Follies tonight! Try out for a part in 'Camp Showdown'." Felice and Teri decided they would both try out for the play.

That night at the try-outs, Felice listened to the director's instructions. Ms. Rule saw how nervous the girls were and said, "Be yourselves because we're here to have fun," she said.

After the tryouts, the cast list was posted. Ms. Rule noticed that Felice looked disappointed because she didn't want to play the villain. Ms. Rule knew how she felt, but told Felice to give it a try, it might be fun.

After they had been rehearsing for awhile, Felice realized Ms. Rule was right. She was having fun playing the villain.

The Big Debut

When I saw the poster about the camp play, I knew it was my chance to make friends at Camp Wildfern. All of the other girls had been campers before, but this was my first year, so I had been feeling lonely. I love being in plays, and I thought that my new pal Teri and I could get parts in this one.

After auditions, Ms. Rule, the director of the play, announced that the play was called "Camp Showdown." It was the tale of rival camps that compete each year in a relay race. Camp U-Turn always triumphs any way they can, so a group from Camp 4-Way teams up to win this year's race. I really wanted to be one of the successful Camp 4-Way campers.

I was nervous, but I figured I did well in the audition. When Ms. Rule posted the cast, I was disappointed. I was cast as the captain for the Camp U-Turn team, and I didn't want the role of villain! Ms. Rule said, "Felice, playing the bad guy might be fun." I wasn't so sure.

Once we started rehearsing, I found out that she was right. Any part is a challenge, and I had a great time playing the role.

Checking Comprehension

1. What kind of person is Felice? How can you tell?

   _____

   _____

2. Do you think that Felice would do well in most new situations?
   Why do you think so?

   _____

   _____

Practicing Comprehension Skills

Fill in the circle next to the correct answer.

3. Who is telling the story "Star Struck!"?
   ○ Felice   ○ an outside narrator   ○ Teri   ○ Ms. Rule

4. From what point of view is "Star Struck!" told?
   ○ first-person point of view   ○ third-person point of view

5. What clues in the story "Star Struck!" helped you answer items
   3 and 4?

   _____

   _____

6. From what point of view is "The Big Debut" told?

   ○ first-person point of view   ○ third-person point of view

7. What clues in "The Big Debut" helped you answer item 6?

   _____

   _____

   _____

Rewrite these sentences from Felice's point of view.

8. Ms. Rule told Felice that she should speak more loudly.

   _____

9. She and Teri were happy that they were in the play.

   _____

Rewrite this sentence so that a character outside of the story is talking about Felice and the campers.

10. We worked hard to memorize our lines.

   _____

Practicing Vocabulary

Choose a word from the box that best completes each sentence.

audition	campers'	cast	director's	rehearsing	rival	villain

11. Rico went to the _____ for the play.

12. Rico hoped for the part of a hero, not a _____.

13. Rico ended up _____ as a thief.

14. Camp Wildfire competes with a _____ camp.

15. The _____ choice for the part was final.

16. Once we start _____, Rico will be practicing his part every day.

17. He hopes to hear the other _____ applause.

Writing a Character Sketch
On another sheet of paper, write two descriptions of the same character. Use first-person point of view in one and third-person in the other. Ask a partner to identify the point of view in each.

Text Structure

Authors try to write in a clear and organized way. In fiction, authors will usually organize a story's events in order from beginning to end. In nonfiction, authors may organize information about real people, events, and things in different ways. The chart shows some ways nonfiction writing can be organized.

Sequence	Events or steps in a process are presented in the order they happen, often using clue words such as *first, then, after, finally*.
Cause and Effect	What happens and the reasons why things happen may be explained. Clue words are *because, as a result, so*, and *therefore*.
Problem and Solution	A problem is stated, followed by how it was or may be solved.
Compare and Contrast	How two subjects are alike and different is described. Clue words are *like, similar to, on the other hand, however, unlike*, and *different*.

Read the passage. Think about how the information is organized.

For many years, people dreamed of flying. However, no one could figure out how to keep a human body up in the air. In the 1700s, Frenchmen Joseph and Etienne Mongolfier had a good idea. They tried different materials and gases and discovered that a paper and linen balloon filled with hot air from a fire would rise. On November 21, 1783, they sent two men up in a basket attached to a large balloon. Spectators were amazed and excited.

How is this passage organized? Fill in the circle for the answer.

○ sequence   ○ cause and effect

○ problem and solution   ○ compare and contrast

What clues from the text support your answer?

_____

_____

Tip

When you begin reading a story or article, look for how the information is organized. Then it will be easier for you to understand the passage.

Read the following articles about two of the women in the space program. Think about how the writers have organized the facts and ideas.

Ellen Ochoa: Adventures in Space

Ellen Ochoa was the first female Hispanic astronaut. She never expected to be an astronaut, but events in her life led her to that careeer. Ochoa was born in 1958 in Los Angeles and grew up in La Mesa, California. As a child, she wanted to be a professional flutist or a scientist. When she attended graduate school at Stanford University, she finally chose science.

After graduate school, Ochoa worked for a research center. She invented a device that helps scientists inspect distant objects in space by making photographs sharper and clearer.

Before long, NASA (National Aeronautics and Space Administration) noticed and respected Ochoa's accomplishments. In 1990, NASA invited Ochoa to become a member of the U.S. space program. A year later, she became an astronaut, and, in 1993, she flew her first mission on the space shuttle *Discovery*. She flew into space again in 1994. This time she studied the effect of the sun on Earth's atmosphere. In 1999, Ochoa was part of a 10-day mission to deliver supplies to the International Space Station.

Ochoa continues to do research and conduct experiments. She also enjoys talking about the space program and often speaks to groups about her adventures in space.

Mae Jemison: Astronaut with a Mission

Mae Jemison is a scientist, doctor, teacher, and astronaut. She is also the first African American woman to go into outer space.

Growing up in Chicago in the 1960s Jemisen saw how hard it was for poor people to get health care. Because of her experiences, she decided to help others by becoming a doctor. During and after medical school, she focused on the health needs of people in poor countries. As a result, she worked with disadvantaged people in Africa, Asia, and Latin America.

Since childhood, Jemison also wanted to be an astronaut. She returned to the United States and went back to school to take courses she needed for the space program. In 1987, Jemison was accepted for astronaut training. In 1992, she took her first trip into space aboard *Endeavor*, where she conducted experiments to learn more on how living in space affects people's bodies.

Jemison combined her interests in science and space by setting up a satellite system for communicating medical information with countries in West Africa. She has also started an international science camp for teenagers called The Earth We Share so people might become interested in science and space.

Checking Comprehension

1. Why do you think that Ellen Ochoa's invention would be useful to scientists studying planets?

_____

_____

2. How has Mae Jemison's work as a doctor led to better health care for people in poor countries?

_____

_____

Practicing Comprehension Skills

3. Fill in the circle next to the sentence that tells how the writer organizes information in "Ellen Ochoa: Adventures in Space."

   ○ The writer lists problems and solutions.   ○ The writer uses sequence of events.

   ○ The writer compares and contrasts.   ○ The writer lists causes and effects.

4. Complete the time line to organize the main points of the article.

1958	_____
	went to Stanford University
1990	_____
	_____
_____	flew on *Discovery*
1994	_____
_____	part of a 10-day mission
today	_____

5. How does the writer organize information in "Mae Jemison: Astronaut with a Mission"?

   ○ The writer lists problems and solutions. ○ The writer uses sequence of events.

   ○ The writer compares and contrasts. ○ The writer lists causes and effects.

6. What clue words in the passage helped you choose your answer?

   _____

Complete the following statement by writing a cause or an effect.

7. Mae Jemison's concern for the health of poor people was a result of

   _____

Practicing Vocabulary

Choose the word from the box that best matches each clue.
Write the word on the line.

_____	8. including two or more nations
_____	9. machine or tool
_____	10. in a difficult situation
_____	11. achievements
_____	12. honored
_____	13. something that travels around a planet
_____	14. look at closely or carefully

> **accomplishments**
> **device**
> **disadvantaged**
> **inspect**
> **international**
> **respected**
> **satellite**

MAKING THE Reading AND Writing CONNECTION

Writing an Informative Paragraph

On a sheet of paper, write a paragraph about a career that you might like to have. You can organize your paragraph by using sequence, causes and effects, explaining a problem and solution, or comparing and contrasting two career possibilities.

Author's Viewpoint

Every author has opinions, feelings, beliefs, and thoughts about the subjects or ideas he or she writes about. This is called the **author's viewpoint.** To figure out an author's viewpoint, look at the words used and the opinions expressed. Then look for information that supports the author's viewpoint.

Each of the following sentences gives a different viewpoint. What words and phrases in each sentence tell you how the author feels?

Searching for lost treasure is an awesome hobby.

Searching for lost treasure is a waste of time.

In the first sentence, the word *awesome* shows the author thinks searching for lost treasure is a wonderful thing to do. In the second sentence, the words *waste of time* show the author's viewpoint that searching for lost treasure is not worthwhile.

Read the article about a shipwreck. Think about the author's viewpoint.

While diving in the sea near southern Turkey, a diver saw some strange metal objects. The objects turned out to be part of an amazing 3,000-year-old shipwreck. One of the most important items was a bronze sword. The real importance of the shipwreck, though, is the precious information it gives people today about a piece of the past.

Fill in the circle next to the sentence that best describes the author's viewpoint about the shipwreck.

○ The shipwreck is only interesting to divers.

○ The shipwreck is important for teaching us about the past.

○ The shipwreck is just a collection of old, useless items.

○ The shipwreck is like all other shipwrecks.

Write three words that show the author's viewpoint.

_____

> **Tip**
>
> When you read, look for words that are clues to the author's thinking, opinions, and beliefs. Such word clues can help you figure out the author's viewpoint.

Read the article about a lost treasure found at sea. As you read, look for words and phrases that are clues to the author's viewpoint.

The Treasure of the Whydah

When Barry Clifford was a boy, his uncle told him stories about a ship called the *Whydah*. Legends said that the *Whydah* disappeared on April 26, 1717. It was believed to have sunk in the waters off Cape Cod, Massachusetts, near where Barry lived. The ship's captain, Sam Bellamy, had been traveling with his crew from England to Africa to the West Indies. Captain Bellamy had gathered a fortune in gold and silver coins and African jewelry, but this wealth had gone down with the ship.

His uncle's tales fascinated Barry, who thought it would be exciting to search for the *Whydah*. In high school, Barry decided that he would someday find the lost treasure. It was a dream he never gave up, even when others said it was nonsense.

When Barry was an adult, he began his search, spending nearly all his money on a boat and diving gear. After years of diving and exploring the ocean floor, Barry finally discovered a cannon and a pile of gold and silver coins.

Scientists believe his discovery is the wreck of the *Whydah*. They think it may turn out to be worth hundreds of millions of dollars.

Since his discovery, Barry has been uninterested in riches. He hasn't sold any of the 100,000 items he found in the shipwreck. Instead, he has paid scientists to study the wreck and to protect its remains. He also opened a museum to share the treasures from the *Whydah* with the public. One expert has called Barry Clifford's discovery fascinating, especially the masses of African gold and carpenter's tools from long ago.

The real treasure of the *Whydah*, however, is not the gold and the other riches that were found at the bottom of the sea. What is most valuable about the discoveries is the lessons they have to teach us. Thanks to Barry Clifford and his determination, we better understand what life may have been like long ago.

Checking Comprehension

1. Why do you think Barry Clifford has not tried to make money by selling the treasures?

   _____

   _____

2. Why do you think it took years for Barry Clifford to locate the wreck of the *Whydah*?

   _____

   _____

Practicing Comprehension Skills

3. Write a sentence to describe the author's viewpoint in "The Treasure of the *Whydah*."

   _____

   _____

4. What words in the passage helped you figure out the viewpoint?

   _____

Fill in the circle next to the words that complete the statement.

5. Based on the passage, the author thinks that Barry Clifford is
   - ○ selfish and greedy.
   - ○ determined and hard-working.
   - ○ someone who gives up easily.
   - ○ easy to trick.

6. What information supports your answer to item 5?

   _____

   _____

   _____

7. Fill in the circle before the sentence that best describes the author's viewpoint about the legend of the *Whydah*.

○ The legend about the *Whydah* is boring.

○ Barry's uncle told him stories about the shipwreck that were untrue.

○ The *Whydah* legend is exciting and leads people to make discoveries.

○ Listening to shipwreck legends is a good way for people to get rich.

8. What phrases support your answer to item 7?

_____

_____

Practicing Vocabulary

Write a word from the box that completes each analogy.

| expert | fortune | gear | jewelry | nonsense | uninterested | valuable |

9. *Materials* are to *supplies* as _____ is to *equipment*.

10. *Wood* is to *furniture* as *gold* is to _____.

11. *Beginner* is to *unskilled* as _____ is to *skilled*.

12. *Wealth* is to _____ as *property* is to *possessions*.

13. *Horrible* is to *wonderful* as *cheap* is to _____.

14. *Arrived* is to *landed* as _____ is to *silliness*.

15. *Calm* is to *upset* as *attentive* is to _____.

MAKING THE Reading AND Writing CONNECTION

Writing a Paragraph
On a separate sheet of paper, write about an activity you really enjoy or dislike. Use words that show your viewpoint and information that supports it. Ask a partner to identify your viewpoint.

Making Generalizations

Sometimes you read ideas about several things or people. If these things have something in common, you can use what you have read and what you already know to make one statement, or **generalization,** about all of them. It explains what people, animals, or things are like most of the time. A generalization often uses a clue word such as *most, many, usually, all, few, always, never, some,* or *generally.*

Valid or true generalizations are based on facts. **Faulty** or false generalizations do not have enough factual support to make them correct. Here's an example: **Poodles are wonderful family pets.** Some poodles may not be wonderful pets, so this generalization is faulty. Adding the word *most* or *many* makes the generalization valid: **Most poodles are wonderful family pets.** Knowing how to judge and how to make generalizations will help you better understand and explain what you read.

Read the article. Look for generalizations. Also notice if the author supports the generalizations.

People generally think household pets are the only dogs. Yet the dog family, or canids, include wolves, coyotes, foxes, and jackals too.

All canids eat meat. Most canids that hunt for prey live in well-organized social groups called "packs." The pet dog's pack is its human family.

Fill in the circle before the sentence that is a generalization.

○ Pet dogs are just part of the dog family, or canids.

○ People generally think pets are the only dogs.

Read the following generalization based on the article. Decide if it is valid or faulty and tell why.

All meat-eaters are members of the dog family.

_____

> ### Tip
> A generalization is a statement that tells how several things or people are alike in some way. Words such as *most, usually, generally,* and *many* often signal generalizations.

Read the article about dogs. Look for generalizations the author makes. Then think about generalizations that you can make.

Dog Heroes

The collie with the golden and white coat barks until a man opens the door. The dog barks again, tilting her head to show that she is listening to something far away. "What's the matter, Lassie? Is someone in trouble?" the man asks. Lassie barks again, as if saying, "Yes, someone needs help. Follow me!"

This scene is from a movie, and the dog is Lassie, a famous animal actor. Lassie began starring in movies in 1943 and later starred in a television show. All viewers loved watching the clever and heroic dog! Lassie rescued people in danger and performed other daring feats. The dogs that played the role of Lassie over the years were all males descended from the first Lassie, a male collie named Pal. Every Lassie learned to bark, tilt his head, give a pleading look, and perform many different commands.

Many people think it's impossible for real-life pet dogs to act like heroes, but they are wrong! Since 1900, the American Humane Association has ensured that heroic animals are recognized by giving awards to animals for their bravery.

Pet pigs won awards in 1984 and 1996, and cats have won several times, but the pets that win most often are dogs. Dogs have won honors for saving people in many different situations and for protecting them from robbers. One winner was Merle, a golden retriever who rescued a person from drowning in icy water. Another was Lady, a Boston terrier who was bitten by a rattlesnake while protecting a two-year-old child. A dog named Foxy won for alerting a neighbor that her owner had fallen.

When people are endangered by fire, dogs have come to the rescue. Many of the association's winners have saved people from burning buildings. One example was Spuds, a Dalmatian who not only awakened his sleeping owner but also carried a kitten out of the burning building. A Rottweiler named Eve pulled her owner to safety from a van that was about to explode in flames.

Can real-life pet dogs act as heroically as the trained animals in movies? The answer is yes!

Checking Comprehension

1. What made Lassie different from other pet dogs?

   _____

   _____

2. Why do you think dogs such as Merle, Lady, Foxy, Spuds, Eve, and others are able to act so heroically?

   _____

   _____

Practicing Comprehension Skills

These statements are based on information from "Dog Heroes." Fill in the circle next to each statement that is a generalization.

3. ○ Lassie was a collie with a golden and white coat.

   ○ Lassie performed in movies and on television.

   ○ Lassie began starring in movies in 1943.

   ○ Lassie always acted in response to commands.

4. ○ Brave Lassie performed heroic feats.

   ○ The first Lassie was a male collie named Pal.

   ○ Some real-life dogs are as heroic as Lassie.

   ○ Pigs won bravery awards in 1984 and 1996.

5. What facts support your answer to item 4?

   _____

   _____

6. What kinds of pets win the bravery awards? Write a generalization to answer the question.

   _____

Read each pair of generalizations. Circle the faulty one. Then rewrite the faulty generalization so it is valid.

7. All viewers loved watching the heroic and clever Lassie! Every Lassie learned to perform a variety of different behaviors.

    Valid Generalization:

    _____

8. Some pet dogs have saved people from drowning. When people are endangered by fire, dogs come to the rescue.

    Valid Generalization:

    _____

Practicing Vocabulary

Write a word from the box to finish each sentence.

alerting	daring	ensured	feats	heroically	honors	impossible

9. Our dog's shyness has _____ us that she will never be brave.

10. Most of the _____ Cassie does are funny rather than heroic.

11. Maybe Cassie could win _____ for being the funniest dog.

12. It would be _____ for Cassie to come out from under the bed.

13. It's _____ to believe Cassie could be an aggressive dog.

14. Acting _____ is not the way Cassie behaves.

15. Cassie is best at _____ us to an empty food dish.

Writing an Informative Paragraph
With your classmates do a class survey about what animals they like best. Think of some generalizations about the survey. Then use another sheet of paper to write a paragraph telling about your class's favorite animals.

Literary Elements: Character

Characters are the people or animals in stories. Sometimes authors tell you directly what characters are like by naming their character traits. Other times, authors include details that help you form your own ideas. An author may describe a character, tell what a character says and does, and show the thoughts and reactions of other characters. Sometimes characters say or think things that help you decide what other characters are like. Figuring out what characters are like can help you predict how they will respond to events in a story.

Read the story. Look for clues that tell about the main character, Zeke.

The neighborhood kids heard Zeke banging in his garage. "What's Zeke doing now?" asked Valerie. "He's always busy with something, but today he's noisier than usual! I'd say strange events are about to happen."

"He says he's building an airplane," said Will. "My father gave him a broken lawn mower. You know Zeke—he can make something out of anything!"

"Zeke bought six loaves of bread and a gigantic jar of peanut butter," said Donny. He wondered nervously what Zeke's vivid imagination was doing with these ordinary things.

Just then they heard a thunderous noise as something came crashing out of the garage. All the kids saw was Zeke's determined, red face under his wild, curly hair. "I'll send postcards!" Zeke bellowed boldly as he ascended into the clouds.

Fill in the circle before the words that tell about Zeke.

○ imaginative   ○ adventurous   ○ quiet   ○ nervous

What clues from the story tell you what Zeke is like?

_____

_____

_____

_____

Tip

To learn about a character, ask yourself, "What does the character say and do? How do the author and other characters describe the character?"

On Your Own

Read the story. As you read, pay attention to how the characters act and how they behave toward each other. What do these clues tell you about each character?

Mina's Marvelous Mess

As Tony strolled into the kitchen, he noticed his sister Mina cooking something in her small tabletop oven. Mina wrinkled her nose and frowned in frustration.

"What is it?" asked Tony. "It smells kind of weird."

"I think it's supposed to be sponge cake," said Mina, "but I'm not positive."

Tony peeked into the oven and saw a cake pan in the shape of a dinosaur about to gurgle over with a goo-like substance. It looked like melting green plastic wrap.

"It smells like it should be thrown away in the garbage disposal in the kitchen sink," said Tony.

"Well, it says right here, 'Sally's Superior Sponge Cake.' I suppose the cookbook could be wrong," Mina said, squinting at the page.

"Did you follow the directions?" asked Tony as the little cake began to ooze.

"Mostly," said Mina.

Just as the cake was about to spill over, Tony grabbed a potholder and pulled the pan out of the oven. He set it on the counter and poked at it. It felt like a rubber eraser.

"What did you do, exactly?" asked Tony.

Mina put her hands on her hips and said, "Well, I didn't measure the milk perfectly, so everything was kind of juicy. I put in more flour, but it got lumpy, so I put in a tiny bit of water. That was a giant mistake. Then I added instant pudding mix to make it thick, which worked perfectly."

"Instant pudding mix?"

Mina nodded. "Pretty ingenious, don't you think? The only flavor we had in the cupboard was pistachio, though, which is why it came out kind of greenish. The frosting will cover it up."

"I don't think you want to frost this," said Tony. "Entomb it instead."

Mina began to think Tony was right.

"Wait a second," said Mina, as she carefully cut around the edge of the pan and popped the dinosaur out onto a plate. She bent the neck a little and straightened one leg, but the dinosaur held its position. "Look how cool this is! It's like rubber play clay. If I make a whole bunch of these, I can use them to set up a display for my Prehistoric Life science report!"

"That's a great idea," said Tony. "I'll help you. Do you think you can goof up the recipe again?"

"That will be a piece of cake," said Mina.

Checking Comprehension

1. What details tell you that the cake-baking project is not going well?

    _____

    _____

2. How can you tell that Mina is an inexperienced but creative cook?

    _____

    _____

Practicing Comprehension Skills

3. How would you describe Mina? List at least three character traits.

    _____

4. Use the graphic organizer to support your answer to item 3. In
    the middle box, write your answer to item 3. In the outer boxes,
    write things that Mina says and does and things that Tony says or
    does that show you what Mina is like.

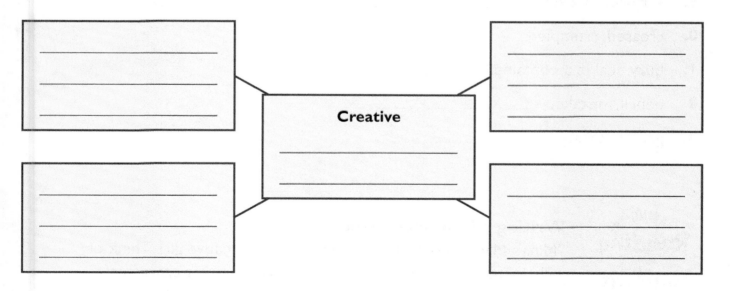

Read each question. Fill in the circle next to the correct answer.

5. What does Tony do that shows he is helpful?
- ○ He peeks into the oven to look at the cake.
- ○ He pulls the pan out just before it spills over.
- ○ He tells Mina to throw the cake away.
- ○ He pokes at the cake.

6. How can you tell that Tony cares about his sister?
- ○ He tells her she has a great idea and offers to help.
- ○ He is not interested in what is sister is doing.
- ○ He tells Mina to bury her project.
- ○ He asks her what she did wrong.

Practicing Vocabulary

Write the word from the box that belongs in each group.

disposal	entomb	eraser	ingenious	positive	squinting	wrinkled

7. sure, certain, _____

8. garbage can, trash bin, _____

9. very smart, clever, _____

10. creased, crumpled, _____

11. bury, seal in a container, _____

12. pencil, mistake, _____

13. gazing, staring, _____

Writing a Character Sketch
"Mina's Marvelous Mess" tells about an imaginative girl. Think of a character you have met in a story and a trait that character has. On a separate sheet of paper, write a character sketch that describes how the character shows the trait.

Literary Elements: Plot

In the beginning of a story, you learn about the characters and the setting. Important events follow which almost always center around a goal or problem. These events are called the **plot.** The plot is made of different parts.

Conflict	a problem or goal that characters must solve or reach
Rising Action	the action as the characters try to solve the problem
Climax	the exciting point when the characters face the conflict
Resolution	the end or outcome of the story that shows what happened after the problem was solved or the goal reached

As you read, think about the important events in the story.

Jessie and Taylor sat at Jessie's kitchen counter planning a tree-planting ceremony. "We have shovels, a camera, and snacks," Taylor said, checking her list.

"We don't have a tree to plant!" Jessie exclaimed. "I totally forgot to phone the nursery, and the ceremony is tomorrow! What are we going to do?"

The bewildered girls noticed Jessie's neighbor, Mr. Campos, digging up several trees.

"Mr. Campos!" Jessie called, dashing outside. "Would you be willing to donate your trees to a worthy cause?"

The next day, Taylor and Jessie were proud. They had four trees for the ceremony instead of one!

Think about the plot of the story as you answer the questions.

What is the problem in this story?

_____

What happens at the story's climax?

_____

Tip

Follow the plot of a story by asking yourself, "What is the problem or goal at the beginning of the story? What events lead to solving the problem or reaching the goal? How does the story end?"

As you read the story about a newspaper recycling project, think about the story events that are important in the plot.

LOTS OF NEWS

by Joyce Annette Barnes

Ethan Honeywell stacked the carefully bound newspapers into his father's van. For weeks, Ethan had pulled a wagon around the neighborhood, collecting papers for the recycling drive. "We're delighted to help," his neighbors said when Ethan explained how fourth graders all over town were involved in the project. Nothing distracted Ethan from his goal because the school that collected the most newsprint would receive a new computer.

On the morning of the contest, Ethan's father said, "Let's go weigh in." A sign at the recycling center proclaimed, "Fourth Grade Recycling Contest. Prizes Awarded Today!" Ethan's jaw dropped when he saw all the cars and vans brimming with newspapers. His teacher waved to him from the crowd as Ethan joined his classmates to watch load after load of newspapers—some lighter, some heavier—nudge the needle across the scale.

Finally it was Ethan's turn to weigh in. "You worked hard, son. I'm proud of you whether your school wins or not," said his dad. Ethan managed a grin, but his heart was pounding. He crossed his fingers as the needle moved past 50, past 100, past even 125 pounds. He had gathered more than 140 pounds of newspapers!

"Way to go, Ethan," cheered the Jefferson students. Ethan watched closely as the last entrants weighed in. Finally a loudspeaker declared the decision. "The prize for the biggest load gathered goes to . . . Jefferson School!" All the students erupted into cheers as the principal stepped forward to collect the prize. Ethan could hardly hear the announcement that came from the loudspeaker next. "We also have a prize for the individual who brought the biggest load. The prize for the heaviest load goes to Ethan Honeywell."

"What? I . . . I didn't know kids were getting prizes too!" he stammered. His father patted him on his back and pushed him toward the judges' area.

Grinning, Ethan collected his prize, a gift certificate to his favorite store. Tomorrow, he'd cruise the neighborhood on the new skateboard he had been attracted to in the store window. He'd be sure to thank his neighbors for being such devoted readers.

Checking Comprehension

1. How did Ethan act and feel when it was his turn to weigh in his collection of newspapers? What does this tell you about him?

   _____

   _____

2. At the beginning of the story, how did you think the story would end? Did it end the way you predicted it would? Explain.

   _____

   _____

   _____

Practicing Comprehension Skills

Use the following graphic organizer to show the plot of "Lots of News." Start with the Problem.

5. Climax: _____

   _____

   _____

4. Rising Action:

   _____

_____

_____

_____

6. Resolution (Outcome): _____

   _____

   _____

3. Problem (Goal): _____

   _____

   _____

Read each of the story events. If the event is important to the plot of the story, write **Yes** on the line. If the event does not move the plot of the story along, write **No** on the line.

7. _____ The neighbors were delighted to help Ethan.

8. _____ For weeks, Ethan collected papers for the recycling drive.

9. _____ Ethan's teacher waved to him from the crowd.

10. _____ A loudspeaker announced that Jefferson School had won.

11. _____ The loudspeaker announced that Ethan had won a prize, too.

Practicing Vocabulary

Write the word from the box that has a meaning similar to the underlined word in the sentence.

attracted	certificate	declared	devoted	distracted	entrants	recycling

_____ 12. All of the <u>contestants</u> stood in a line.

_____ 13. They had been <u>lured</u> to the unusual art contest.

_____ 14. One contestant was <u>preoccupied</u> with looking at the sky.

_____ 15. Her statue made of rolled newspapers was described as "<u>reusing paper</u>."

_____ 16. It takes a <u>constant</u> recycler to collect 140 pounds of newspapers.

_____ 17. Finally, they <u>announced</u> the winner.

_____ 18. The newspaper artist got her <u>award</u> as it started to rain.

Writing a Dialogue

On a separate sheet of paper, write what two characters say to each other about a problem that they have in school and how they want to solve it. Then use what you wrote to describe the plot of a story.

Literary Elements: Setting

Have you ever read a story that took you to a time and place you have never been before? Where and when a story takes place is called the **setting**. The setting can be a real time and place, or it can be imaginary. A story's setting can take place in the present, the past, or the future. As you read a story, look for details that help you figure out where and when the story takes place. Also ask yourself: Is the setting important to this story? How would the story be different if it happened in another time and place?

When you figure out a story's setting, think about how it affects the characters. If the setting is dark and scary, then the characters are likely to be anxious and afraid. If the setting changes, a character's feelings or reactions might change, too.

Read the passage. What is the setting?

"I can't wait to get there," said Coletta on the long drive to Bryce Canyon for a summer vacation. Too excited to sit quietly, Coletta fidgeted and chattered. She asked her parents countless times, "Are we there yet?"

At last the family stood at the canyon rim. Hundreds of rust-colored spires rose from below. Coletta knew that wind, ice, and rain had worn away stone to form the shapes, but it seemed as if giant sculptors had created a fairy-tale city.

"How do you like the view?" asked Coletta's father.

Coletta was completely speechless.

Write answers to the questions on the lines.

Where and when does the story take place?

_____

How does the setting of the story affect Coletta?

_____

_____

Tip

As you read, look for clues that help you figure out when and where the story takes place. Then think about how the setting influences the characters' feelings and actions.

Read the story about space travelers. Think about the setting and how it influences what the characters think and do.

The Unwelcome Committee

"Descend when ready," ordered Commander Pawlis in the spacecraft *Traveler*. Explorers Shannon and Louis dropped a portable staircase from the hovering exploration vehicle and climbed down to the surface of the planet. This planet had an oxygen-rich atmosphere, but would it resemble their home planet, Earth?

The pair surveyed the scene as an orange sun glowed in a golden-white sky. Yellow sand covered everything, forming shallow valleys and low hills. "Nothing could live here," said Shannon.

"Then what—or who—are they?" asked Louis, squinting and pointing. At the top of a distant rise loomed three figures, taller than any beings the explorers had ever seen.

"They seem to be a welcome committee," Louis remarked. "Shall we say hello?"

Louis and Shannon plodded through the sand to meet the committee. After an hour, the figures didn't seem to be any nearer, but explorers never give up, so Louis and Shannon walked on.

"Those three haven't moved," said Louis.

"One of them has a larger head than the others," said Shannon.

"Maybe it's the leader," said Louis.

When Louis and Shannon were nearly upon the three figures, they realized that the shapes were constructed of stone. The explorers burst out laughing, as Shannon cried, "They look so lifelike! I wonder how these stones were made."

"Wind, probably," replied Louis. At that instant, the wind began to blow, whipping up a solid wall of yellow dust and hurling it against the explorers. Louis and Shannon stumbled, and the giant hand of the wind shoved them across the sand. They curled into balls, pulling their shield capes around them, as the wind bounced them at high speed, screaming into their ears.

Suddenly the wind ceased and the air lay silent and still. The explorers stood up and shook themselves off. Louis pointed with surprise to their ship—somehow, the explorers were back at their starting point. Without any hesitation, they ascended quickly into the exploration vehicle. They would report to Commander Pawlis that this planet was dry, dusty, and much too windy to be like any place on Earth.

Checking Comprehension

1. Why are Louis and Shannon exploring the planet?

   _____

2. The explorers conclude that the planet is dry, dusty, and much too windy to be like any place on Earth. Do you agree? Why or why not?

   _____

   _____

Practicing Comprehension Skills

Write the answer to each question on the lines.

3. When does this story take place: in the past, the present, or the future? Give reasons for your answer.

   _____

   _____

4. Reread "The Unwelcome Committee." Find details about the planet setting and write them on the spokes of the web.

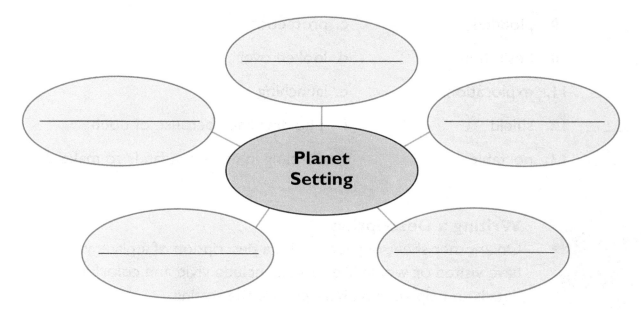

5. How does the setting affect what the characters do and think?

_____

_____

_____

6. Use the details from your web to write a description of the strange planet so that someone can picture it clearly.

_____

_____

_____

_____

Practicing Vocabulary

Match the word on the left with the word or words on the right that means the same thing. Write the letter on the line.

_____ 7. surveyed	a. walked heavily
_____ 8. hurling	b. movable
_____ 9. plodded	c. protection
_____ 10. hesitation	d. looked over
_____ 11. exploration	e. launching
_____ 12. shield	f. a holding back because of doubt
_____ 13. portable	g. traveling in unknown lands to make discoveries

Writing a Description

On another sheet of paper, write a description of a place you have visited or would like to visit. Include vivid and colorful details to help your readers picture the setting.

Literary Elements: Theme

Every story has a message the author wants you to understand. This message is the **theme**. You could also say that the theme is the "big idea" of the story. This big idea is usually about life. For example, the author may want you to understand that friendship is valuable or that help can come from unexpected sources. Usually there's more than one way to state a story's theme. You might say that a story's message is that "Friendship is valuable," while someone else would say, "People need other people."

Sometimes the author states the theme directly. More often, you have to figure out the theme. To do that, pay attention to story events and the characters' goals and actions towards those goals.

Read the passage. Think about the "big idea."

In ancient Greece, a traveler returned to Athens after visiting many foreign lands. One of the tales he told was of the awesome things he had witnessed and experienced on the island of Rhodes. "I competed in a jumping contest there," he said proudly, "and I jumped a distance that no one could beat. Just go to Rhodes and ask them, and they will relate the story of my wonderful jump."

One doubtful listener spoke up, saying, "Why must we travel to Rhodes to learn of your fantastic jump? You can demonstrate it for us right here in Athens if you just imagine that this is Rhodes and make your jump!"

Fill in the circle next to the sentence that best states the theme of the story.

○ People at home know you best.

○ Be proud of your athletic ability.

○ If you brag, be ready to prove your words.

○ Travelers are never happy at home.

Tip

To identify a story's theme, think about the events and the characters' goals and actions. Then ask yourself, "What big idea or message does the author want me to understand?"

Read this folk tale about a contest between a deer and a rabbit. Think about the story's theme.

HOW THE DEER GOT HIS ANTLERS

Long ago, Deer had no antlers. His head was as smooth as a fawn's velvety skin. Deer was also a very swift runner, just as Rabbit was a great jumper. They were both very proud of their abilities and spent every day running and jumping to stay in shape. Deer never said much about his skill, but Rabbit frequently and loudly boasted about what he could do. The other animals argued about which one was faster.

To settle the argument, the animals arranged a race between the two. As a prize for the winner, the animals constructed an elaborate pair of beautiful antlers. Both Deer and Rabbit wanted to have them.

To make the race as hard as possible, the animals set it up through a large boundary of thick bushes. Deer and Rabbit were to start together on one side, push through the bushes, race to and around a large tree, and then come back again. The one who came out of the bushes first would win the antlers.

On the day of the race, all the animals gathered and placed the antlers on the ground to mark the start. Rabbit said, "I don't know this part of the forest; I want to look at the bushes where I am to run."

The animals thought that would be all right, so Rabbit was allowed to head into the bushes. Meanwhile, Deer waited patiently.

Rabbit was gone for so long that the animals suspected he might be up to one of his tricks. They sent Mouse to look for him. Mouse found Rabbit gnawing down plants and pulling them away from under the bushes so he would have a clear path. Deer, who was much taller than Rabbit, would not be able to use Rabbit's path.

The other animals frowned when they heard what mischief Rabbit was up to. When Rabbit finally returned, they accused him of cheating. At first he denied it, but then admitted it when they all went into the bushes and found the cleared path.

The animals immediately awarded the antlers to Deer, who has worn them proudly ever since. Rabbit was told that since he was so fond of hiding in the bushes and gnawing on plants, he might as well do that all the time. To this day rabbits are timid and spend most of their time hiding in bushes. Thankfully, they can still jump quickly, because that's what they do when they are scared by something.

Checking Comprehension

1. Why do the animals plan a race?

    _____

    _____

2. Why did the animals decide that Rabbit was a trickster?

    _____

    _____

Practicing Comprehension Skills

Fill in the circle next to the best answer.

3. What goal did both Rabbit and Deer have?

    ○ to trick the other animals   ○ to settle the argument

    ○ to get the antlers   ○ to cheat in the race

4. Which sentence best states the theme of the story?

    ○ A contest can solve an argument.   ○ Cheaters never win.

    ○ Rabbits are tricky.   ○ Deer are fast runners.

5. Which story event helps you figure out the theme?

    ○ Long ago, Deer did not have antlers.   ○ Rabbit secretly cleared a path through the bushes.

    ○ Deer and Rabbit would race through a patch of bushes and back again.   ○ Some animals thought Rabbit could jump as fast as Deer could run.

6. What is another way to state the theme? Write your answer.

    _____

    _____

7. Think about Deer's actions in the story. What message do you think the storyteller wants you to understand from Deer's actions? Fill in the circle.

○ It doesn't pay to wait around while others trick you.

○ Patience is rewarded in the end.

○ The best runner doesn't always win the race.

○ The better the prize, the harder the race is.

8. What happens to Rabbit at the end of the story? What big idea does this make you think about? Write your answer.

_____

_____

Practicing Vocabulary

Choose the word from the box that best replaces the underlined word or words. Write the word on the line.

accused	allowed	antlers	denied	gnawing	suspected	boundary

_____ 9. The animals met at the <u>edge</u> of the bushes.

_____ 10. The prize was a pair of fine <u>horns</u>.

_____ 11. The creatures <u>believed</u> Rabbit was playing a trick.

_____ 12. Rabbit was not <u>permitted</u> to take part in the race.

_____ 13. "I was <u>blamed</u> so unfairly! The fault is not mine!"

_____ 14. Rabbit, the trickster, <u>said he'd not done</u> the crime.

_____ 15. Mouse found Rabbit <u>chewing</u> on bushes.

Writing a Story
On another sheet of paper, write a one-page story about people or animals that contains a message, or big idea. Trade stories with a partner. Take turns figuring out the themes.

Synonyms

Imagine that someone offered you a dish of your favorite ice cream. Would you prefer the ice cream that was creamy or velvety? The words *creamy* and *velvety* have similar meanings. Words with similar meanings are called **synonyms.**

Authors try to choose synonyms to show an exact meaning. They may also use synonyms to avoid using the same word over and to make their writing more interesting. Sometimes authors use synonyms to explain an unfamiliar word as in this sentence:

> **The chocolate ice cream was scrumptious, the most delicious I had ever had.**

Knowing about synonyms can help you understand and enjoy what you read. Synonyms can also help you improve your writing.

Read the passage. Look for synonyms.

"I scream! You scream! We all scream for ice cream!" People all over the world have loved ice cream for a long time.

Nobody knows exactly where this frozen treat originated or who invented it. Chinese people combined milk and fruit ices long before the European visitor Marco Polo discovered these sweets in the late 1200s. He then introduced the flavored ice, or sherbet, to people back home in Europe. They immediately adored it. About 400 years later, an unknown chef decided to try something a little different. Instead of putting the ice into the mixture, the chef used the ice to chill the blend of sweetened, flavored milk. Ice cream was born!

Tip

Synonyms are words with similar meanings. To decide if two words are synonyms, ask yourself if they have almost the same meaning.

Reread the article to find two more synonyms that belong in each group. Write the words on the lines.

liked, enjoyed, _____, _____

discovered, created, _____, _____

dessert, tidbit, _____, _____

As you read the following article about ice cream cones, look for synonyms. Think about why the author chose particular words.

Who Put the Ice Cream into the Cone?

There's nothing as delicious as an ice cream cone on a hot summer day. Everyone enjoys tasting the cool, velvety ice cream and munching the sweet cone. Whoever invented the ice cream cone surely deserves an award!

The prize could go to Ernest Hamwi, or to Arnold Fornachou, or maybe to Italo Marchiony, or to . . . As you may guess, there is more than one story about who first put ice cream into a cone.

The best-known legend credits Ernest Hamwi, an immigrant to the United States from Syria. Hamwi was a baker, one of the many food vendors at the St. Louis World's Fair in 1904. There were millions of hungry fairgoers stopping at the food stands. Hamwi was selling a Middle Eastern pastry similar to a thin, crisp waffle. Nearby was an ice cream vendor named Arnold Fornachou. Back then, ice cream was sold in small, inexpensive dishes.

One day, the ice cream vendor ran out of dishes. How could he sell ice cream? Hamwi helpfully rolled one of his pastries into a horn shape and plopped a scoop of ice cream into it.

The combination of ice cream and pastry was the perfect match. Soon ice cream eaters strolled the fairgrounds nibbling the crunchy treat.

A second version of the legend says that Arnold Fornachou came up with the idea. The story says he used Hamwi's pastries to create the first waffle cone.

If Hamwi or Fornachou invented the ice cream cone, then why did Italo Marchiony receive a patent, or sole right, to sell ice cream cones before the World's Fair even opened? Marchiony sold ice cream in New York City in the late 1800s. Instead of selling ice cream in the customary dishes, Marchiony placed the ice cream in a cup-shaped pastry. He patented his invention of the mold for baking the pastry.

Despite all the discussion, there is no agreement about the one true inventor of the cone. There is a general acceptance, however, that ice cream cones became a big hit only after the St. Louis World's Fair.

Checking Comprehension

1. What did Ernest Hamwi do to be considered a possible inventor of the ice cream cone?

   _____

   _____

2. Why might Italo Marchiony, more than Ernest Hamwi, be viewed as the real inventor of ice cream cones?

   _____

   _____

Practicing Comprehension Skills

Each word below was used in the article about ice cream. Next to the word, write a synonym from the box that might have been used in its place.

award	created	tasty	placed	account
pairing	crisp	sellers	newcomer	cheap

3. version _____

4. prize _____

5. delicious _____

6. plopped _____

7. match _____

8. crunchy _____

9. invented _____

10. vendors _____

11. immigrant _____

12. inexpensive _____

Read the following sentences. Fill in the circle in front of the word that is a synonym for the underlined word.

13. There were millions of <u>hungry</u> fairgoers.

    ○ satisfied   ○ angry   ○ starving   ○ cheerful

14. Ice cream eaters <u>strolled</u> the fairgrounds nibbling the crunchy treat.

    ○ marched   ○ walked   ○ hopped   ○ observed

15. Reread the article to find three synonyms for *eating*. Write each synonym in one of the ovals in the web below.

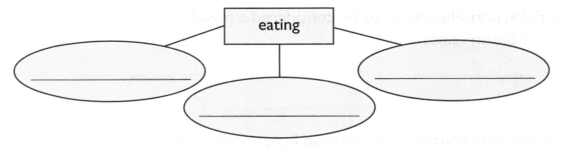

16. Write other synonyms you can think of for the word *eating*.

_____

Practicing Vocabulary

Choose the word from the box to finish each sentence in the paragraph.

pastry	acceptance	customary	invention	inexpensive	legend	patented

17.   Carrie started working on her dog-walking _____ as

soon as she got up in the morning. She didn't even take time to eat

her breakfast _____. Carrie was tired of walking her dog

in the _____ way like everyone else in the neighborhood

did. She chose _____ materials to keep costs low. After it

was _____, she would be able to sell it everywhere. As

she worked, Carrie wondered how long it would be before her device

had a general _____ among dog walkers. She dreamed

that she would become a _____ among inventors.

Writing a Descriptive Paragraph
On another sheet of paper, write a description of your favorite food. Choose just the right words to tell how the food tastes, looks, and smells. Be sure to include synonyms.

Antonyms

Look out the window, and what do you see? Do you see a neighborhood in the city or the country? Is the weather sunny or cloudy? Is it day or night, winter or summer? The world is full of opposites. When two words have opposite meanings, they are called **antonyms.** *City* and *country* are antonyms. So are *sunny* and *cloudy,* and *summer* and *winter.*

Knowing about antonyms can help you understand what you read. You can also find just the right words to describe things when you write. Using antonyms in your writing helps readers understand differences.

Read the article. Notice how antonyms can help you understand this passage about the sidewinder.

While many desert snakes are harmless, the sidewinder is deadly. Pale in color and up to 32 inches long, this rattlesnake has a short, dark stripe on its head. Unlike most snakes, which are smooth, the sidewinder has rough scales that help it move sideways in S-shaped loops. This rapid "sidewinding" helps the snake travel quickly over the scorching desert sand.

Sidewinders are well-adapted to the desert's dryness. Some never drink water but always get the moisture they need from their prey. When the day is very hot, sidewinders stay underground. When it is cool at night, they go aboveground to hunt.

Reread the paragraphs to find the antonym for each word listed below. Write the antonym on the line.

ANTONYMS		**ANTONYMS**	
harmless	_____	long	_____
pale	_____	hot	_____
smooth	_____	day	_____
never	_____	underground	_____

> **Tip**
>
> Antonyms are words with opposite meanings. When you find antonyms in a paragraph, think about the differences they describe.

Read the article about the desert. Look for antonyms the writer used to point out differences.

Surviving the Desert

Because the desert air is dry, clouds rarely form and the sun usually scorches the air and the ground. Even in the shade, temperatures can soar to 130° F. That's hot! During the cloudless night, the desert heat escapes into space. Then temperatures may drop below freezing. Few animals can cope with such searing and chilling temperatures. However, the animals that live in the desert have found amazing ways to survive.

While some animals dread the heat, others welcome it because they are well-adapted to deal with it. Coldblooded reptiles can absorb a certain amount of heat. Similarly, the camel and ostrich, although warmblooded, can stand a rise in body temperature that might harm others. Many animals are light colored to reflect the sun's rays. Others, like the jackrabbit, have large ears that radiate excess heat.

To survive the heat, most desert animals avoid it. They spend the day under stones or in burrows. Only in the cool of dawn or dusk or in darkness, do they come out to scamper around looking for food and water.

A source of water is just as important to desert survival as finding ways to stay cool. One source is the dew that forms after the quick drop in desert temperatures at night. Insects drink the dew directly. Larger animals take in dew in a roundabout way while eating plants.

Despite adaptations, searching for water is an endless activity for many desert animals. That's why it's so important for desert animals also to have ways to conserve water. The hard, horny coverings of scorpions and spiders, for example, are waterproof, and so are the soft scales of reptiles. These animals do not waste water by sweating or panting.

By spending the day in small burrows, some desert animals create a moist atmosphere with their breath. Animals such as gerbils store dry seeds in their burrows. While the animals sleep, these seeds absorb moisture from the animal's breath. Then the animals eat the seeds when they awaken. In this way, they regain water.

Checking Comprehension

1. Why is "Surviving the Desert" a good title for the article?

   _____

   _____

2. Describe how three animals in the article are adapted to desert life.

   _____

   _____

   _____

   _____

Practicing Comprehension Skills

Circle the word in each sentence that is an antonym for the underlined word.

3. Because the desert air is dry, clouds rarely form and the sun usually beats down.

4. In the cool of dawn or dusk, the animals come out to find food.

5. Few plants and animals can cope with these searing and chilling temperatures.

6. The animals are able to regain some of the water that they would otherwise lose.

Complete the sentence by choosing the antonym for the underlined word. Fill in the circle by the correct answer.

7. Most desert animals dread the heat. Others _____ it.
   ○ dislike   ○ welcome   ○ adapt   ○ escape

8. Temperatures soar in daytime and _____ at night.
   ○ rise   ○ drop   ○ survive   ○ cope

9. Some animals absorb the sun's heat. Those with light coats _____ it.
   ○ measure   ○ reflect   ○ ignore   ○ conserve

10. Read each word below. Look back at the article and find an antonym for the word. Write it on the line.

   freezes _____   slow _____

   conserve _____   coldblooded _____

   directly _____   moist _____

Practicing Vocabulary

Choose the word from the box that matches each clue. Write the word on the line.

cloudless	dew	dread	endless	cope	excess	survival

_____ 11. water drops on plants

_____ 12. deal with

_____ 13. extra

_____ 14. going on forever

_____ 15. fear

_____ 16. sunny

_____ 17. staying alive

MAKING THE Reading AND Writing CONNECTION

Writing a Description
On a separate sheet of paper, write a paragraph comparing and contrasting two places you have visited or know about, such as a desert and a forest. Use antonyms to show readers some of the differences between the two places.

Using Figurative Language

Can an orange taste like sunshine? Can the full moon be a silver dollar? Is thunder ever angry? The answer is yes when you use **figurative language.** Figurative language gives words a meaning beyond their everyday definitions. When you read figurative language, it can help you see things in a new way.

Similes, metaphors, and personification are three kinds of figurative language. A **simile** compares two unlike things using the word *like, as,* or *than:* **The orange juice tastes like a glass of sunlight.** A metaphor compares two unlike things without using *like, as,* or *than:* **The Milky Way is a diamond necklace made of stars.** Personification gives human traits to objects or animals: **The angry thunder growled in the stormy sky.**

As you read this passage about ants, look for figurative language.

A single leafcutter ant is so small, it's almost invisible. It appears as a red dot on the ground. When it's time to gather leaves, though, an army of leafcutters can cover the forest floor like a carpet. Each ant carries a leaf back to the nest. The leaf is as heavy for the ant as a 600-pound weight would be for a human! This tiny worker never complains about its heavy work. After dropping off its burden, the leafcutter hastens back for another load. For these insects, leafcutting season is a marathon race!

Read each item below. Complete the chart by writing what each item is compared to.

a single leafcutter	_____
an army of leafcutters	_____
_____	a marathon race

What human trait does the author give to the ants?

_____

> ## Tip
> When you read, use figurative language to help you picture what the author describes. Similes and metaphors make comparisons. Giving a human trait to animals or objects is personification.

Poems are often rich in figurative language. Read this poem.
Think about the poet's use of figurative language.

Carrying

by Reeve Lindbergh

What can I carry, and what carries me?
I can't carry a maple or sycamore tree.
But a tree carries me in its branches and leaves,
With green, growing arms, like a garden with sleeves.

I can carry things out if I fashion a plan.
I can't carry an automobile in my hand,
But a road carries me and my car, as we ride
Over ribbons of roads through the whole countryside.

Deep down inside me I carry a dream.
I can't carry a river, or even a stream.
But a stream carries me and my dream joyfully,
Like a big, bubbling bathtub that flows to the sea.

When I sing to myself, I can carry a tune.
I can't carry Earth, I can't carry the moon.
But the universe carries the moon, me, and Mars,
In a chorus of worlds, twirling planets, and stars.

Big things carry little things, I know they do.
(And small things, like ants, carry bigger ones, too.)
But I'm noticing lately how often I see
That the things I can't carry CAN carry me!

Checking Comprehension

1. What is the main idea the poet expresses in the poem "Carrying"?

    _____

    _____

2. How does a tree "carry" the poet?

    _____

    _____

Practicing Comprehension Skills

Fill in the circle next to the best answer for each question.

3. What human trait does the poet give to a tree in lines 1–4?

    ○ A tree grows a garden.   ○ A tree has arms.

    ○ A tree has branches.   ○ A tree wears clothes.

4. In line 8, the poet compares roads with ribbons. This metaphor suggests that roads

    ○ are usually brightly colored.   ○ are long and twisting.

    ○ are often tied up.   ○ are velvety and shiny.

5. Read these lines from the poem. Underline two things being compared. Write the kind of figurative language the poet is using to compare these things. Then write the meaning of the figurative language.

    But a <u>stream</u> carries me and my dream joyfully,

    Like a big, bubbling <u>bathtub</u> that flows to the sea.

    _____

    _____

Read the following lines from the poem. Then answer the questions.

> But the universe carries the moon, me, and Mars,
>
> In a chorus of worlds, twirling planets, and stars.

6. What kind of figurative language does the poet use in these lines?

   _____

7. What does she compare? She says _____

8. What does the figurative language help you see in a new way?

   _____

   _____

Practicing Vocabulary

Write a word from the box to finish each comparison or analogy.

sleeves	chorus	countryside	fashion	sea	twirling	universe

9. *Sand grains* are to a *beach* as *stars* are to the _____.

10. *Legs* are to *pants* as _____ are to *coats*.

11. *Spinning* is to _____ as *walking* is to *strolling*.

12. *Mountain* is to *hill* as _____ is to *lake*.

13. *Singers* are to _____ as *marchers* are to *parade*.

14. *Make* is to _____ as *jump* is to *leap*.

15. *Fields* are to _____ as *buildings* are to *cityscape*.

Writing a Poem
On another sheet of paper, write a poem about something in nature that has surprised you or made you think. Use similes, metaphors, and personification to paint word pictures.

Connotation and Denotation

Would you rather be called *curious* or *nosy*? Both words have a similar dictionary meaning, or **denotation**. They both mean "to be interested in something." Even so, you would probably rather be called *curious*.

Words with similar denotations can have different connotations. A **connotation** is the good or bad feeling that a word suggests. The word *curious* has a good or positive connotation. Curious people learn and discover new things. *Nosy*, however, has a bad, or negative connotation. It usually suggests people who want to know things that are none of their business.

Some words do not have a connotation. Readers don't have a positive or a negative feeling about them. Thinking about the connotations of words will help you better understand what you read and will help you identify the opinions of authors based on the words they choose.

Read the article about a president and his pets. Look for words with similar denotations but different connotations.

During the 1920s, Calvin Coolidge was President. A bashful man, he rarely said a word. His wife Grace, who was less timid, told reporters that the Coolidges liked animals. Soon people began shipping them pets. At first, the traditional dogs and cats arrived. Later the pets were less common. Lion cubs, a bear, and even a small hippo were sent to the White House! The President adored a frisky raccoon named Rebecca. He built a special house for her and walked her when she got overactive.

Write two words from the passage that have the same or a similar denotation as each word listed below. Then circle the word with the most positive connotation.

shy _____ _____

usual _____ _____

loved _____ _____

> ## Tip
>
> The denotation of a word is its dictionary meaning. A positive connotation of a word suggests good feelings, images, and memories. A negative connotation suggests unpleasant feelings.

STRATEGY: Identifying Connotation and Denotation   **101**

On Your Own

As you read the article about pets in the White House, think about the word choices the author makes and the positive and negative connotations of the words.

WILD White House Pets

Pets are no strangers to the White House. Many of America's presidents have been animal lovers. In recent times, White House pets have been tame dogs, cats, and ponies. Long ago, however, presidential pets, like our nation itself, were wilder!

In 1806, President Thomas Jefferson resided in the White House. Passersby often commented on his pet grizzly bears. Explorers had discovered these fierce bears, captured a pair of cubs, and sent them to Jefferson. While the President was excited about his cubs, his enemies in Congress constantly mocked the outlandish pets, calling the White House "The President's Bear Garden."

By 1825, the bears were long gone from the White House scene. Now the mansion was home to President John Quincy Adams and his alligator. The green beast actually belonged to General Lafayette, a French hero who had helped the United States win the Revolutionary War. When Lafayette asked Adams to keep the alligator for him, the President couldn't refuse.

While President Adams babysat the huge reptile, First Lady Louisa Adams was busy raising thousands of silkworms. Always a thrifty woman, Mrs. Adams used the silk from the worms' cocoons to make cloth for her gowns.

When President Martin Van Buren moved into the White House in 1837, he brought his tiger cubs with him. At least, Van Buren said the tigers were his. The Sultan of Oman had sent the tigers when Van Buren was elected, so Congress argued that the cats belonged to the American people. A fight over the tigers continued for months. Eventually, Congress sent someone to capture the tigers and put them in a zoo.

Twenty years later, President James Buchanan received another incredible gift. This time, the King of Siam sent a herd of elephants! Buchanan had no desire to share his mansion with the big creatures, so he sent them to the zoo. Buchanan did, however, keep another gift—a pair of bald eagles. They were a fitting symbol of presidential power.

Checking Comprehension

1. How did most of the presidents mentioned get their unusual pets?

   _____

2. What similar political effect did Jefferson's bears and Van Buren's tigers have?

   _____

   _____

Practicing Comprehension Skills

Draw a line from the word in the first column to a word in the second column that has almost the same denotation. Then, in the space before each word write a **P** for the word with the more positive connotation, and **N** for the word with the more negative connotation in each pair.

3. _____ thrifty   _____ opponents

4. _____ continued   _____ crazy

5. _____ enemies   _____ cheap

6. _____ excited   _____ laughed

7. _____ mocked   _____ raged on

The words under each sentence have a denotation that is similar to the underlined word. Fill in the circle in front of the word with the most *positive* connotation.

8. While President Adams <u>babysat</u> the huge reptile, First Lady Louisa Adams was busy raising thousands of silkworms.
   ○ guarded   ○ minded   ○ watched   ○ tended

9. Eventually, Congress sent someone to <u>capture</u> the tigers and put them in a zoo.
   ○ seize   ○ snatch   ○ claim   ○ nab

The words following each sentence have a denotation that is similar to the underlined word. Fill in the circle in front of the word with the most *negative* connotation.

10. Explorers had discovered these <u>fierce</u> bears.
  ○ savage   ○ angry   ○ mean   ○ wild

11. President James Buchanan received another <u>incredible</u> gift.
  ○ amazing   ○ outlandish   ○ fantastic   ○ wondrous

12. Buchanan had no desire to share his mansion with the big <u>creatures</u>.
  ○ beings   ○ animals   ○ beasts   ○ mammals

Practicing Vocabulary

Match the word on the left with the word or words on the right that means the same thing. Write the letter on the line.

_____ 13. argued   a. hard to believe

_____ 14. herd   b. turn down or say no

_____ 15. mocked   c. a person, place, or thing that stands for something else

_____ 16. incredible d. fought or disagreed

_____ 17. symbol   e. a place where something happens

_____ 18. refuse   f. a group of animals

_____ 19. scene   g. made fun of

MAKING THE
Reading
AND
Writing
CONNECTION

Writing a Persuasive Paragraph
On another sheet of paper, write a persuasive paragraph to convince someone to do something to help animals. Work with a partner to list words you could use with positive and negative connotations.

Using Maps

Imagine that you are planning a trip to an interesting place in your area. You have never been to this place. How could you find it? You could use a **map**. There are many different kinds of maps. One kind of map that would help you find a place is a **road map.** A road map is a drawing that shows and names the roads, streets, and landmarks in a certain area.

A road map uses a **compass rose** to show the directions north, south, east, and west. Many maps also use **symbols** to show the locations of important buildings and other places. A map key, or **legend,** tells what each symbol means.

Read the excerpt from a brochure about a building in Denver. Look at the map as you read.

Just blocks from the state capitol building in Denver, Colorado, stands the Denver Mint. Half of all the coins in the United States are manufactured here. That's 38 million coins a day. The Mint offers free tours, which cover the entire minting process. You can watch new coins being counted and bagged as they pour from stamping machines.

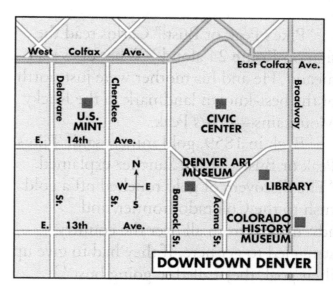

Use the map to answer these questions. Fill in the circle next to the correct answer.

Which street is just north of the Denver Mint?

○ E. 14th Street ○ West Colfax Avenue

○ Acoma Street ○ Bannock Street

Which building is at the corner of 13th Avenue and Broadway?

○ Denver Art Museum ○ Civic Center

○ Library ○ Colorado History Museum

Tip

A road or street map can help you find places in a certain area. Symbols used to mark places on a map are usually different from one map to another. Always check the legend to see what a symbol stands for.

As you read the story about a trip to Pike's Peak, find Carlos's location on the map.

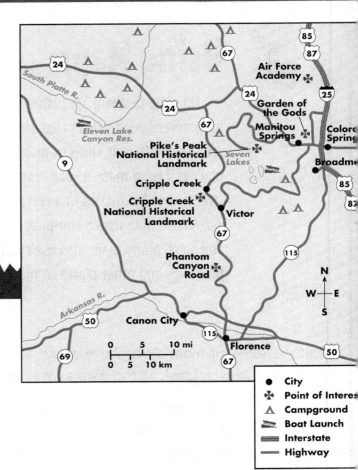

Pike's Peak and Bust

"Pike's Peak or Bust!" Carlos read the sign on Route 24 aloud. "What does that mean?" He and his mother were just north of the best-known landmark in the Rocky Mountains—Pike's Peak.

"Back in 1859, gold miners said, 'Pike's Peak or Bust,' " Mrs. Sanchez explained. "The discovery of gold touched off a gold rush to the Colorado frontier, and adventurers from all over the country struggled to get here. If they had to give up their goal, they called it 'going bust.' "

The road they were on ran right to the top of Pike's Peak. Mrs. Sanchez and Jake planned to drive the whole way, but that was not to be. Near the foot of the mountain, their car made a strange sound, then quit and rolled to a stop.

Using her cell phone, Mrs. Sanchez called for a tow truck to pull the car to Manitou Springs. "It's fixable," the mechanic at the car repair shop announced after inspecting the engine. "I should have it finished by late afternoon."

"Late afternoon!" Carlos moaned. "We were going to drive up Pike's Peak."

"Why not take the cog railway?" the mechanic suggested. "Pike's Peak is the only mountain in Colorado that has one. It's a nine-mile scenic ride, and a lot of people say it's very pleasurable. I can get my helper to drop you off at the station."

Less than an hour later, Mrs. Sanchez and Carlos were 14,110 feet above sea level, the highest point in Colorado. "If you look east, you can see Kansas 165 miles in the distance!" Mrs. Sanchez exclaimed.

"Pike's Peak and Bust!" Carlos shouted into the wind. "Our car went bust, but we made it anyway!"

Checking Comprehension

1. Why is Pike's Peak an important landmark?

   _____

   _____

2. What is the meaning of the title "Pike's Peak and Bust"?

   _____

   _____

Practicing Study Skills

Look at the map to answer the questions. Fill in the circle next to the correct answer.

3. How many points of interest are between Florence and Cripple Creek on Route 67?

   ○ two   ○ four   ○ three   ○ five

4. Which point of interest is closest to Pike's Peak?

   ○ Garden of the Gods   ○ Air Force Academy

   ○ Phantom Canyon Road   ○ Cripple Creek Historical Landmark

5. On the map, which body of water does not have a boat launch?

   ○ Arkansas River   ○ South Platte River

   ○ Seven Lakes   ○ Eleven Lake Canyon Reservoir

Write the correct answer on the line.

6. How many times does Route 24 cross the South Platte River? _____

7. Is Cripple Creek west or east of Manitou Springs? _____

8. If you were traveling north on Route 67 from Florence, what would be the first town you would come to?

   _____

For each statement, write **True** or **False** on the line.

9. Route 67 runs generally in a north-south direction. _____

10. The map shows no campgrounds on the south bank of the

    South Platte River. _____

11. The map shows a point of interest on Route 115 near

    Florence. _____

Practicing Vocabulary

Write the correct word next to each clue. The letters in the boxes
spell the way to reach Pike's Peak.

adventurers	fixable	frontier	mechanic	pleasurable	scenic	station

12. pretty to look at ___ ___ ___ ___ ___ ___

13. enjoyable ___ ___ ___ ___ ___ ___ ___ ___ ___

14. the edge of a settled area ___ ___ ___ ___ ___ ___ ___ ___

15. person who fixes cars ___ ___ ___ ___ ___ ___ ___ ___

16. not broken forever ___ ___ ___ ___ ___ ___ ___

17. place for trains ___ ___ ___ ___ ___ ___ ___

18. people who ___ ___ ___ ___ ___ ___ ___ ___ ___ ___
    like exciting trips

How can you reach the top of Pike's Peak? _____

Writing an Advertisement

Choose an interesting place in your town. On a sheet of paper,
write an advertisement and include a map. Label the streets,
include a compass rose, and use symbols to show places.

Understanding Tables

When you read nonfiction, you usually read for information. You may sometimes find information in picture form. One type of picture that gives information is a **table.** Authors use tables to list and sort information in a way that is clearer and easier to read and understand than a description or an explanation. Tables also help you to compare and contrast information.

Finding information on a table is easy. A table arranges words and numbers in rows and columns. First, read the title and headings. They tell about the information in the table. Then read down the columns and across the rows to find the information you are looking for.

Read the passage and the table.

Meet the world's biggest mammal, the blue whale. The largest one on record weighed approximately 200 tons. This is heavier than 30 elephants! Besides being the heaviest mammal, the blue whale is also the longest. At birth, an infant blue whale is 6 to 8 feet in length. When fully grown, this massive creature can be 100 feet long.

Big Mammals of the World			
Animal	**Weight**	**Height/Length**	**Life span**
Blue whale	400,000 pounds	100 feet long	50+ years
African elephant	12,000 pounds	11 feet tall	about 70 years
Hippopotamus	8,000 pounds	15 feet long	about 60 years

Tip

Read the title and headings of a table first. Then read down the columns and across the rows to find specific information.

Use the passage and the table to answer these questions.

What does the table tell you about the blue whale that you did not learn in the passage?

_____

Which of the three largest mammals lives longest?

_____

Read the article about small mammals. Study the table to help you understand the ideas in the article.

THE 🌎 WORLD'S SMALLEST MAMMALS

From big blue whales to small brown bats, all mammals share a few important characteristics. For one thing, they are vertebrates, meaning that each has a backbone and bony skeleton for support. Mammals are also warmblooded, so that their body temperature stays fairly constant, no matter what the surrounding air or water temperature. Most all land mammals have hair or fur on their bodies. Whales, too, have a few scattered hairs that grow on the snout, chin, and top of the head. Finally, most female mammals give birth to live young and make milk to feed them.

Mammals come in all shapes and sizes. Most of the mammals that people are more familiar with, such as horses, dogs, and cats, are huge when compared with the really small ones. The pygmy white-toothed shrew, for example, is only 1 1/2 inches long, which is about the length of a paper clip. A native animal of Africa, the pygmy shrew looks similar to the other 245 species of shrews found around the world. Shrews look a lot like mice, but they have longer and narrower noses.

Until recently, scientists thought the pygmy shrew was the smallest mammal. Then they discovered the bumblebee bat, a native animal of Thailand that measures just 1 1/4 inches long and weighs 1/20 of an ounce. Because its rain forest habitat is quickly disappearing, there are few bumblebee bats left, making it an endangered species. As a species, however, bats are numerous. Around the globe, another 1,000 species of bats can be found. They are the only mammals that fly.

In general, the smallest mammals tend to be rodents that eat seeds, roots, and leaves. The world's smallest mouse is the pygmy mouse. Only slightly heavier, the shrew mole is the second smallest.

Small Mammals of the World			
Animal	**Weight**	**Length**	**Life span**
Bumblebee bat	1/20 ounce	1 1/4 inches	about 5 years
Pygmy shrew	1/15 ounce	1 1/2 inches	up to 18 months
Pygmy mouse	1/4 ounce	body, 2 inches; tail, 1 inch	a few months
Shrew mole	1/3 ounce	body, 1 inch; tail, 1 inch	3–5 years

Checking Comprehension

1. What would the diet of a newborn blue whale and a newborn bat have in common?

   _____

   _____

2. The bumblebee bat was only recently discovered and is considered endangered. What conclusion can you draw about other species from this information?

   _____

   _____

Practicing Study Skills

Use the passage, "The World's Smallest Mammals," and the table to answer each question. Fill in the circle next to the correct answer.

3. How much does the pygmy mouse weigh?
   - ○ 1/15 ounce
   - ○ 1/4 ounce
   - ○ 1/3 ounce
   - ○ 2 ounces

4. Which small mammal is the shortest?
   - ○ pygmy shrew
   - ○ pygmy mouse
   - ○ bumblebee bat
   - ○ shrew mole

5. How many kinds of shrews are there?
   - ○ 1,000
   - ○ 245
   - ○ 112
   - ○ 120

6. Which two mammals have life spans that are nearly the same?
   - ○ bumblebee bat and shrew mole
   - ○ bumblebee bat and pygmy shrew
   - ○ pygmy mouse and shrew mole
   - ○ shrew mole and pygmy shrew

Write **True** or **False** next to each statement.

7. _____ Most mammals make milk for their young.

8. _____ Instead of giving birth to live young, some mammals lay eggs.

9. _____ Mammals are coldblooded.

10. Suppose you were to see a pygmy shrew and a pygmy mouse at the zoo. How could you tell them apart?

_____

_____

Practicing Vocabulary

Write a word from the box on each line to finish the paragraph.

| characteristics   habitat   mammals   vertebrates   recently   rodents   similar |

11.   From whales to bats, _____ come in all shapes and sizes. Because they have backbones, mammals are _____. One of the main _____ that makes all mammals _____ is that they are warmblooded. Mammals make their homes in nearly every _____ on Earth. One of the most _____ discovered mammals is the bumblebee bat in Thailand. Bats are the second largest group of mammals after _____.

MAKING THE Reading AND Writing CONNECTION

Creating a Table
On another sheet of paper, write a report about an animal group that interests you or that you have studied. As part of your report, include a table. Use headings such as name of animal, color, length, habitat, and life span.

Using Graphs

A **graph** is a kind of picture that shows information. Instead of reading sentences containing lots of numbers, you can use graphs to quickly find information and to compare things.

One kind of graph is a **bar graph.** To read a bar graph, start with the title to find out what information is shown. Then read the labels. Words will tell you what things are being compared. Numbers will tell you how fast, how big, or how many, depending on what the graph is about. The bars on a bar graph may be horizontal (left to right) or vertical (top to bottom). Sometimes you may see a **double bar graph.** On a double bar graph, bars are shown next to each other. They are used to compare different numbers for the same item.

Read the paragraph. Use the bar graph to compare information.

Immigrants are people who leave their home country to move to a new country. The bar graph compares the number of immigrants that came to the United States from each country listed in 1995 and 1998.

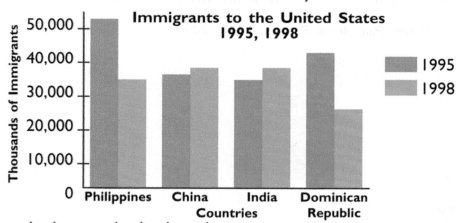

Tip

Think about the information that you want to learn as you read a graph. To help you decide what number a bar shows, place your finger on the top of a bar and move it left or down to find a number.

Using the bar graph, check each true statement.

_____ In 1995, more immigrants came from China than from India.

_____ The number of immigrants from the Dominican Republic fell between 1995 and 1998.

_____ The fewest immigrants in 1998 came from India.

Read the article about the population of the United States. As you read, study the bar graph to compare information.

Tracking Population Changes

How do we know how many people live in the United States? Does someone actually count them one by one? The answer is yes, though the someone is the United States Bureau of the Census, a government agency. An official count of the population is called a census. A census is scheduled every ten years, as required by the U.S. Constitution.

The Census Bureau publishes data, or numerical information, that shows who is living where. This data can be used to identify what changes are happening in the American population. One type of change in the late twentieth century was the growth in different regions.

In addition to counting people every ten years, the Census Bureau also watches growth patterns and makes projections. That means they estimate how fast the population will grow in each state. For example, California's population in 1990 was 31,589,000. The Census projects it will grow to 34,441,000 in 2005. This projection is only an estimate. It is based on how fast the state is growing now.

Seven Most Populous States, 1990, 2005

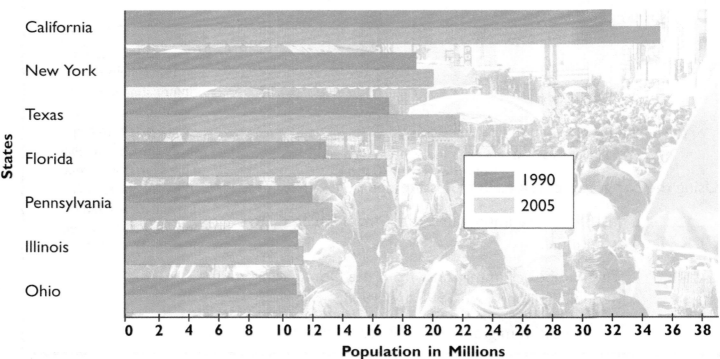

States: California, New York, Texas, Florida, Pennsylvania, Illinois, Ohio

Legend: 1990, 2005

Population in Millions
0 2 4 6 8 10 12 14 16 18 20 22 24 26 28 30 32 34 36 38

Checking Comprehension

1. Why is the job of the U.S. Census important?

   _____

   _____

2. The Census Bureau can only project what a state's future population may be. What does this mean could happen?

   _____

Practicing Study Skills

Complete each sentence with information from the bar graph.

3. The state with a population close to 13 million in 1990 was _____.

4. The state with the largest population in 1990 was _____.

5. Together, Florida and _____ in 1990 nearly equaled California in population.

6. The population of Pennsylvania in 2005 will be almost _____.

Fill in the circle next to the correct answer.

7. Which state will be the largest in population by 2005?
   - ○ Illinois
   - ○ Texas
   - ○ California
   - ○ Florida

8. Which state may be the slowest growing by 2005?
   - ○ New York
   - ○ Illinois
   - ○ Pennsylvania
   - ○ Ohio

9. About how many people might Pennsylvania gain between 1990 and 2005?
   - ○ 1 1/2 million
   - ○ 3 million
   - ○ 5 million
   - ○ less than 1 million

Write **True** or **False** for each statement.

_____ 10. Between 1990 and 2005, New York's population will probably increase by less than two million people.

_____ 11. Florida had a larger population than Texas in 1990.

_____ 12. Illinois and Ohio will have nearly the same population in 2005.

_____ 13. Illinois had more people than Texas in 1990.

_____ 14. The top seven most populous states will all gain population by 2005.

Practicing Vocabulary

Write a word from the box on each line to complete the paragraph.

agency	census	data	watches	projections	population	publishes

15. Once every 10 years, people all over the U.S. must take part in a _____. A government _____ called the United States Bureau of the Census is responsible for doing this. The government tries to count everyone to find out the exact _____. The census takers also gather _____ on the age, race, and income of people. The government _____ books filled with the information gathered. The Census Bureau also _____ growth patterns and makes _____ about the future.

Creating a Bar Graph
Work together to take a survey to find out how many students are in each class in your school. Use a separate sheet of paper to create a bar graph using the information you have gathered. Show number of students along one side and classes along the other.

Using a Dictionary

When you read a word you don't know, use a **dictionary** to help you. A dictionary is a book that lists words in alphabetical order along with their meanings. To find a word, use the **guide words** at the top of each page. They show the first and last **entry words** on a page. Each entry shows the word divided into syllables and how to pronounce the word. Then comes the part of speech, which is usually abbreviated, such as *n.* for *noun* and *v.* for *verb*. The rest of the entry contains the word's meaning or meanings. Using a dictionary helps you to understand what you read and use and spell words correctly when you write.

Have you ever heard about a place called Stonehenge? Read the following passage and look at the photograph.

Standing alone on a plain in England is a group of more than a hundred huge stones called Stonehenge. No one really knows who put the stones there. Many people believe they have been there for about 6,000 years. What was their purpose? Archaeologists have made many guesses, but no one knows for sure.

Read the following dictionary entry.

entry word and syllabication

pronunciation

part of speech

definition

ar·chae·ol·o·gist (är´kē äl´ə jist) **n.** an expert in archaeology, the science that studies ancient times and ancient peoples through the digging up of what is left of ancient cities, tombs, etc... **An archaeologist works to dig up the hidden story of the past.**

example sentence

> ## Tip
> A dictionary will help you learn unfamiliar words. If a word has more than one definition, reread the sentence with each possible meaning. This will help you choose the correct meaning.

How many syllables does *archaeologist* have? _____

What part of speech is the word? _____

Read the article about a mysterious group of statues on a South Pacific island.

Mystery in Stone

Easter Island is a small island in the Pacific Ocean. Its nearest neighbors are a thousand miles away. Many people visit Easter Island to see and marvel at the moai (mow-eye), which are huge sculptures that were carved almost 2,000 years ago. They are constructed of dark red volcanic rock. Long ago, three volcanoes erupted where Easter Island stands today, forming the island when the molten lava from the volcanoes cooled into rock. This rock is soft enough to carve with simple tools.

More than 800 moai stand erect on the desolate island. The average moai is 13 feet tall and weighs almost 14 tons. Some are only 3 feet tall while others stand 70 feet tall! They face away from the sea, as if they are protecting the island's people.

No one knows exactly how the statues got there or even why they are there. One idea is that the moai were made for the chiefs who used to live on the island. The chief would have hired an artist to carve the stone and had his family help to pay for the statue by feeding the stone carver and his team while they worked.

Once the moai were finished, they had to be dragged along dirt roads. This would have taken a tremendous amount of muscle power. The Easter Islanders probably secured the bodies of the statues with ropes, then used rollers to move them along the ground. Another possibility is that the people used the smooth backs of the stone figures to slide them along. After the figures were in place, the statues' heads were raised and positioned on top.

In 1722, the statues amazed the first Europeans to land on Easter Island. People today still visit to study the figures, or just to look. All are awed by these impressive sculptures.

Did people worship the moai? Were the moai built to honor the dead? No one theory has been proven. Even the people who still live on the island can't say for sure. The statues are still one of the great mysteries of the world.

Checking Comprehension

1. What is the mystery that surrounds Easter Island?

   _____

   _____

2. Describe what you would see if you were to tour the moai on Easter Island.

   _____

   _____

Practicing Study Skills

Use the dictionary entries to answer the questions. Fill in the circle next to the correct answers.

awe (ô), **1** *n.* a feeling of fear or wonder caused by something beautiful or powerful: *The sight of the mountain filled us with awe.* **2** *v.* to cause to feel awe: *The beauty of the waterfall awed the explorers.* **awed, aw·ing.**

mys·ter·y (mis´ tər ē), **1** *n.* something that is hidden, unknown, or secret: *Astronomers seek out the mysteries of the universe.* **2** something that is not explained or understood: *It is a mystery how they survived the accident.* **3** novel or story about a mysterious event that is not explained until the end. *pl.* mys·ter·ies

3. The entry word *awe* would appear on a page with which of these guide words?

   ○ await/awake   ○ avoid/awful   ○ awhile/axe   ○ award/away

4. The entry word *mystery* would appear on a page with which of these guide words?

   ○ musty/myopia   ○ muzzle/mysterious   ○ mutual/mystify   ○ mystical/myth

5. The word *awed* is used near the end of the article. Reread the sentence. Which meaning of awe is used?

　○ noun definition　　　　　　　　○ verb definition

6. Which meaning of *mystery* is used in the following sentence?

Until recently, black holes in outer space were a mystery.

_____

7. Write a sentence that uses the word *awe* as a noun.

_____

8. Write a sentence that uses the third definition of *mystery*.

_____

Practicing Vocabulary

Write a word from the box that best completes each analogy.

9. *Eye* is to *sight* as _____ is to *movement*.

10. *Lake* is to *land* as _____ is to *water*.

11. *Steam* is to *water* as _____ is to *rock*.

12. *Brushes* are to a *painter* as *knives* are to a _____.

13. *Soap* is to *clean* as *lock* is to _____.

14. *Ballads* are to *songs* as *statues* are to _____.

15. *Pretty* is to *beautiful* as _____ is to *ordinary*.

average
carver
island
lava
muscle
sculptures
secured

Writing Sentences

Find a word in the dictionary that is new to you, has more than one meaning, and can be used as two different parts of speech. Write sentences using each meaning and part of speech.

Using an Encyclopedia

When you need information, an **encyclopedia** is a good place to look. An encyclopedia is a book or set of books with information on many subjects. Each book in a set is called a **volume** and has a number and one or more letters on the spine. Each volume contains articles called **entries** arranged alphabetically.

To find an entry, think of a key word. Suppose you want to know where the 1988 Summer Olympics took place. A good key word to look for is *Olympics*. If you want to look up a person, use the person's last name. People are listed last name first in an encyclopedia. Then find the volume with the letter that begins your subject name. A **guide word** at the top of each page helps you find an entry. The guide words on facing pages list the first and last entries on those pages.

Read the following encyclopedia entry to learn about the beginning of the modern Olympic games. Notice the features.

entry word

guide word

entry

Olympia (Greece)

Olympia (Greece) Olympia is the site of the Olympian Games, which were celebrated by the ancient Greeks. In the 1890s, the ruins of Olympia were found in a valley in Elis, on the west coast of Greece. Scientists discovered that sports festivals were held there 2,000 years earlier. This discovery brought about the formation of the modern Olympic Games, which began in 1896 in Athens, Greece.

How would you find this entry in a set of encyclopedias?

_____

_____

Tip

You can use an encyclopedia on the Internet or on a CD-ROM, or use printed books. All three encyclopedias are used in the same way and have similar features.

Read the encyclopedia entry about an Olympic athlete. Think about other key words you might use to find more information.

Joyner-Kersee, Jackie (1962–   ) An American track and field athlete.

Jacqueline Joyner was born in East St. Louis, Illinois, where she played high school basketball. In 1980 she attended the University of California at Los Angeles on a basketball scholarship. In college Joyner played basketball all four years and also ran track, setting national records.

While still in college, she decided to train for the 1984 Olympics, which would be held in Los Angeles. These games introduced the heptathlon, a seven-event competition that is considered by many to be very difficult. It includes the 100-meter hurdles, high jump, shot put, 200-meter sprint, long jump, javelin throw, and 800-meter run. Joyner entered the heptathlon and won the silver medal.

In 1986, Joyner married her track coach, Bob Kersee. She also gave up basketball to focus on track. With the help of her husband, she made many improvements in her heptathlon skills. In 1987, she won the heptathlon at the Pan American Games.

The 1988 Olympics were held in Seoul, South Korea. For Joyner-Kersee, these games were the fulfillment of her dreams. She won the gold medal for the heptathlon, setting a world record. She won a second gold medal for the long jump, the first American ever to win this event.

The 1992 Olympics were celebrated in Barcelona, Spain. At age 30, Jackie Joyner-Kersee was still unbeatable as she again won the gold medal for the heptathlon. She also placed third in the long jump.

Jackie Joyner-Kersee suffers badly from asthma, a lung disease. Painful leg muscles also bother her. Yet she continues to compete in championships. In 1993 she won her fourth world title for the heptathlon, and in 1994 she set a new U.S. record for the long jump. Many people consider Jackie Joyner-Kersee the world's greatest female athlete.

Jackie Joyner-Kersee

Checking Comprehension

1. How did Jackie Joyner-Kersee's performance in the heptathlon event at the Olympic Games change between 1984 and 1988?

   _____

   _____

2. Why do many people consider Jackie the world's greatest athlete?

   _____

   _____

Practicing Study Skills

3. If you wanted to learn details about Jackie Joyner-Kersee's main Olympic event, which key word would you look up in an encyclopedia?

   _____

4. Would you find information about the Olympic Games in the same encyclopedia volume with the article on Jackie Joyner-Kersee? Explain.

   _____

   _____

5. If you wanted to learn about the track and field event that Jackie Joyner-Kersee won in 1987, which key word would you use?
   - ○ University of California
   - ○ Pan American Games
   - ○ Olympics
   - ○ track and field

6. If you wanted to learn more about the site of the 1992 Olympics, which key word would you use?
   - ○ Seoul, South Korea
   - ○ Barcelona, Spain
   - ○ East St. Louis, Illinois
   - ○ Los Angeles, California

7. Guide words at the top of the pages in an encyclopedia help you find entries. The guide words show the first and last entries on two facing pages. Fill in the circle in front of the guide words you would find on the pages with the entry for Jackie Joyner-Kersee.

   ○ JOURNALISM and JOURNEY

   ○ JOYCE, JAMES and JUAN CARLOS

   ○ JUNGLE and JUPITER

   ○ JONES, JOHN PAUL and JORDAN

Practicing Vocabulary

Write the word from the box that belongs in each group.

fulfillment sprint hurdles meter painful scholarship unbeatable

8. undefeated, unsurpassed, _____

9. aching, sore, _____

10. grant, aid, _____

11. bars, jumps, _____

12. run, dash, _____

13. yard, measurement, _____

14. achievement, completion, _____

Writing a Summary
Think of a topic about the Olympics that you'd like to know more about. Find and read an encyclopedia article about your topic. On another sheet of paper, write a short summary of it.

Level D Glossary

A

acceptance (ak sep´təns) approval

accompanying (əkum´pə nə iŋ) playing music along with

accomplishments (ə käm´plish mənts) tasks that have been successfully completed

accused (ə kyoozd´) blamed someone for doing something wrong

adventurers (ad ven´chər ərz) people who take part in an exciting or dangerous event or activity

agency (ā´jən sē) a part of government or some other organization that gives a special kind of help

alerting (ə lʉrt´iŋ) warning

allowed (ə loud´) let something be done; permitted

ancient (ān´chənt or ān´shənt) very old

announced (ə nounst´) said; told

antlers (ant´lərz) horns on the head of a deer or other related animal

applaud (ə plôd´ or ə pläd´) to show approval or enjoyment of something by clapping the hands

appointed (ə point´əd) named or chosen for an office or position

argued (är´gyood) disagreed; quarreled

assume (ə soom´ or ə syoom´) to suppose something to be a fact; to take for granted

assured (ə shoord´) told or promised in a positive way

attracted (ə trakt´əd) won the attention of

audition (ô dish´ən or ä dish´ən) an opportunity for an actor, singer, or musician to be tested for a job

average (av´ər ij or av´rij) usual

awkward (ôk´wərd or äk´wərd) not having grace or skill; clumsy

B

bloodthirsty (blud´thʉrs´tē) cruel and murderous

boundary (boun´də rē or boun´drē) outside edge or limit

C

campers' (kamp´ərz) belonging to people who vacation at a camp

cargo (kär´gō) load of goods carried by a vehicle

carver (kär´vər) person who makes sculptures by cutting or chipping

cast (kast) the set of actors in a play

census (sen´səs) an official counting to find out how many people there are in a country

certificate (sʉr tif´i kət) an official written or printed statement

characteristics (ker´ək tər is´tiks) parts or qualities that make a person or thing different from others

chorus (kôr´əs) a group of people trained to sing or speak together; any group that moves or sings together

cinch (sinch) something that is easy

citizens (sit´i zənz) people who are members of a country

civil (siv´əl) of a citizen or citizens

clearance (klir´əns) the clear space between two objects

climatic (kli mat´ik) having to do with the usual weather conditions of a place

cloudless (kloud´ləs) without clouds; clear

coaxed (kōkst) urged in a gentle way

coil (koil) something wound in circles

colossal (kə läs´əl) very large or very great

comfortable (kum´fər tə bəl or kumf´tər bəl) giving comfort or ease; pleasant

Constitution (kän´sti too´shən or kän´sti tyoo´shən) the document that contains the basic laws of the U.S.

conversation (kän vər sā´shən) a friendly and informal talk

cope (kōp) to deal with successfully; survive

countryside (kun´trē sid´) the land outside of cities; country

critics (krit´iks) people whose work is judging things, such as books, plays, music, or restaurants

customary (kus´tə mer´ē) according to custom; usual

cyclists (sik´lists or sik´əl ists) people who ride bicycles or motorcycles

D

daring (der´iŋ) bold enough to take risks

data (dāt´ə or dat´ə) facts and figures; information

deadline (ded´lin) the latest time by which something must be done or finished

declared (dē klerd´) said or announced

demonstrate (dem´ən strāt) to show

denied (dē nīd´) said that something is not true or right

describe (də skrib´) tell or write about in some detail

125

desperate (des´pər ət) reckless or careless because one has lost hope

device (dē vɪs´) something made or invented for some special use; a tool or machine

devoted (dē vōt´əd) very loving or loyal

dew (dōō or dyōō) water that forms in little drops on grass, plants, and other things during the night

diameter (di am´ət ər) a straight line that passes through the center of a circle from one side to the other

director's (dər ek´tərz) of or belonging to a person who directs or manages the work of others

disadvantaged (dis´əd vant´ijd) having something that stands in the way of success; handicapped

disposal (di spō´zəl) a machine that grinds garbage so it can be washed down the drain of a sink

distracted (di strakt´əd) drew the mind or attention away to something else

dread (dred) to think about something with great fear or worry

E **eager** (ē´gər) wanting very much; anxious to do or get

endless (end´ləs) having no end; going on forever

ensured (en sho͞or´) made sure or certain

entomb (en to͞om´ or en tyo͞om´) to bury or enclose something in a tomb or grave

entrants (en´trənts) people who take part in a contest

equipment (ē kwip´mənt) all the special things that are needed for some purpose; supplies

eraser (ē rā´sər) a piece of rubber that rubs out pencil marks

errand (er´ənd) a short trip to do something

evidence (ev´i dəns) anything that makes clear or proves something; facts that give a reason for believing something

excess (ek´ses) more than the usual limit; extra

exhilarating (eg zil´ər āt´iŋ) lively; stimulating

experienced (eks spir´ē ənst) having done or lived through something; skilled

expert (eks´pərt) person who has great knowledge or skill in a special area; authority

exploration (eks plər ā´shən) the act of exploring

expression (eks presh´ən) a word, phrase, or saying

extreme (ek strēm´) to the greatest degree

F **farewell** (fer wel´) good wishes when a person leaves; goodbye

fashion (fash´ən) to make, form, or shape

feats (fēts) actions or deeds that show great courage, skill, or strength

fertile (fʉrt´l) able to produce crops

fixable (fiks´ə bəl) able to be repaired

forceful (fôrs´fəl) strong; powerful

fortune (fôr´chən) a large sum of money; wealth

frontier (frun tir´) the part of a settled country that lies next to a region that is still a wild area

fulfillment (fo͞ol fil´mənt) completion

G **gear** (gir) equipment and tools needed for doing something

gnawing (nô´iŋ or nä´iŋ) biting and wearing away bit by bit

H **habitat** (hab´i tat) place where an animal or plant is normally found

harbor (här´bər) to shelter or encourage

harm (härm) to hurt or damage

heftiest (hef´tē ist) heaviest; biggest

herd (hʉrd) number of large animals that live and feed together

heroically (hi rō´ik lē) like a hero; showing great bravery or daring

hesitation (hez´i tā´shən) the act of stopping or waiting because one is not sure

honors (än´ərz) things that are done or given as a sign of respect

hurdles (hʉr´dəlz) small fences or frames that runners or horses must jump over in a certain kind of race

hurling (hʉrl´iŋ) throwing with great force

I **impossible** (im päs´i bəl) not possible; not capable of being done or happening

incredible (in kred´ə bəl) unusual; special in a way that makes it hard to believe

inexpensive (in´ek spen´siv) low in price

ingenious (in jēn´yəs) clever or skillful

injuries (in´jər ēz) harm or damage that is done to a person or thing

inspect (in spekt´) look at carefully; examine

installed (in stôld´) fixed in a position for use

instructed (in strukt´əd) directed; ordered

instrument (in´strə mənt) a device used in making music

international (in tər nash´ə nəl) for or by people in several nations

invention (in ven´shən) something new that did not exist before

investigate (in ves´ti gāt´) to look into so as to learn the facts

island (ī´lənd) a piece of land that is surrounded by water

J

jewelry (jōōl´rē) rings, bracelets, and other ornaments

join (join) to go along with

K

kneaded (nēd´əd) pressed and squeezed with the hands

knowledge (nä´lij) what is known or learned

L

lava (lä´və or lav´ə) hot, melted rock pouring out of a volcano

legend (lej´ənd) story that is handed down through the years

local (lō´kəl) having to do with a particular place

loyal (loi´əl) faithful

M

mammals (mam´əlz) warmblooded animals that have a backbone

mechanic (mə kan´ik) a worker who is skilled in using tools or in making, repairing, and using machines

meter (mēt´ər) the basic unit of length in the metric system, equal to 39.37 inches

misunderstood (mis´un dər stōōd´) understood in a wrong way

mocked (mäkt) made fun of in a rude or mean way

muscle (mus´əl) the tissue in an animal's body that can be stretched or squeezed together to move parts of the body

N

nonsense (nän´sens) speech or writing that is foolish or has no meaning

O

orchestra (ôr´kəs trə) a large group of musicians playing together

P

painful (pān´fəl) hurting

passes (pas´əz) narrow roads or paths

pastry (pās´trē) baked food with a sweet crust

patented (pat´nt əd) got an official document issued by a government that gives a person or company the right to be the only one to make or sell a certain invention for a certain number of years

patience (pā´shəns) the quality of being able to put up with pain, trouble, delay, or boredom without complaining

persisted (pər sist´əd) went on in a stubborn way

personal (pʉr´sə nəl) of one's own; private or individual

physique (fi zēk´) the form or shape of a body

pieces (pēs´əz) parts or sections of a whole, thought of as complete by themselves

pleasurable (plezh´ər ə bəl) causing a feeling of delight or satisfaction; enjoyable

plodded (pläd´əd) walked with effort

pooled (pōōld) put together

population (päp´yōō lā´shən) all of the people who are living in a particular place

portable (pôrt´ə bəl) capable of being carried; easy to carry or move

positive (päz´i tiv) completely sure

possessions (pə zesh´ənz) things a person owns

pouch (pouch) a bag or sack

prey (prā) animals captured for food

projections (prō jek´shənz) predictions made using facts that are already known

protect (prō tekt´) to guard or defend against harm or danger

publishes (pub´lish əs) prints for distribution to the public

R

ravaged (rav´ijd) damaged greatly; destroyed

recently (rē´sənt lē) at a time just before the present time

recreational (rek´rē ā´shən əl) refreshing one's body or mind after working

rectangle (rek´taŋ gəl) a flat figure with four sides and four right angles that is not a square

recycling (rē sī´kliŋ) putting something through a special process so it can be used again

reeled (rēld) pulled in by winding a line

reflected (rē flekt´əd) mirrored

refuse (rē fyōōz´) to reject; to say no

rehearsing (rē hʉrs´iŋ) going through a performance before giving it in public

relatives (rel´ə tivz) people or animals of the same family related by blood or kinship

replied (rē plīd´) answered

reptiles (rep´təlz or rep´tīlz) coldblooded animals that have a backbone and scales, and crawl on the belly or creep on short legs

respected (rē spekt´əd) had a high opinion of

rival (rī´vəl) competing

robot (rō´bät) a machine that is made to work like a human being

rodents (rōd´ntz) animals that have sharp front teeth for gnawing

S

satellite (sat´l īt) a human-made object that has been put into orbit around the earth, moon, or other heavenly body

scene (sēn) the place where something happens

scenic (sēn´ik) having beautiful scenery; pretty to look at

scholarship (skäl´ər ship) a gift of money to help a student pay for instruction

sculptures (skulp´chərz) statues or other objects carved from wood, stone, or other material

sea (sē) the whole body of salt water that covers much of the earth; ocean

secured (si kyōōrd´) tied or fastened in a firm way

segregation (seg rə gā´shən) the practice of forcing people of different racial groups to live apart or go to separate schools

shark (shärk) a large ocean fish that eats other fish and sometimes attacks people

shield (shēld) something that serves as a protective barrier

similar (sim´i lər) almost but not exactly the same; alike

sleeves (slēvz) parts of a garment that cover all or part of the arms

snout (snout) the nose and jaw that stick out from the face of an animal

spacecraft (spās´kraft) any vehicle designed for use in outer space

speedier (spēd´ē ər) faster

sprint (sprint) a short run or race at full speed

squinting (skwint´iŋ) looking with the eyes partly closed

station (stā´shən) a regular stopping place along a route, especially a building at such a place

stockades (stä kādz´) walls of tall stakes built around a place for defense

studied (stud´ēd) looked at or into in a careful way; examined or investigated

sturdier (stʉr´dē ər) stronger

surveyed (sər vād´) looked over in a careful way

survival (sər vī´vəl) the act of continuing to exist in spite of difficulties or danger

suspected (sə spekt´əd) thought of as probably guilty of some wrong action although with little proof

swoop (swōōp) to sweep down or pounce upon suddenly

symbol (sim´bəl) an object that stands for something else

T

talent (tal´ənt) a natural skill that is unusual

traditions (trə dish´enz) customs or beliefs that are handed down

trend (trend) the general direction or course that something takes

trim (trim) to make neat or tidy by cutting or clipping

triumphed (trī´əmft) won; succeeded

twirling (twʉrl´iŋ) turning in a very quick way; spinning

U

unbeatable (un bēt´ə bəl) so good that defeat is impossible

uninterested (un in´trist əd or un in´tər est əd) not interested

universe (yōō´ni vʉrs´) Earth, the sun, stars, and all the things that exist

V

valuable (val´yōō ə bəl or val´yə bəl) thought of as precious, useful, or worthy

vertebrates (vʉr´tə brəts or vʉr tə brāts) animals that have a backbone

video (vid´ē ō´) film

villain (vil´ən) an evil or wicked person

W

watches (wäch´əz or wôch´əz) looks at; pays attention to; observes

wobble (wäb´əl) to move from side to side in an unsteady way

wrinkled (riŋ´kəld) creased

Y

yielded (yēld´əd) produced; gave